"GIVE ME
SERVICE"

"GIVE ME SERVICE"

Keys to Sacred Stewardship

WILLIAM LINN RUTHERFORD

XULON PRESS

Xulon Press
2301 Lucien Way #415
Maitland, FL 32751
407.339.4217
www.xulonpress.com

© 2018 by William Linn Rutherford

All rights reserved solely by the author. The author guarantees all contents are original and do not infringe upon the legal rights of any other person or work. No part of this book may be reproduced in any form without the permission of the author. The views expressed in this book are not necessarily those of the publisher.

Unless otherwise indicated, Scripture quotations taken from the Revised Standard Version (RSV). Copyright © 1946, 1952, and 1971 the Division of Christian Education of the National Council of the Churches of Christ in the United States of America. Used by permission. All rights reserved.

Printed in the United States of America.

ISBN-13: 978-1-54562-779-2

Acknowledgments

Almost every Sunday morning Mom and Dad would prepare their family for church. We all loved our minister, Ray Fenner, but even the smallest in the family, a young boy at the time, knew Mom's joy about going to church involved something more.

One Sunday the boy said he wanted to stay home and play. Mom was not upset or disappointed. Calmly she said, "You can give Jesus an hour of your time."

"But why?" he complained.

"Get ready, we don't want to be late," she answered. And off to church they went, again.

Later when he was eight or nine years old, he entered the front door of the church with his family, and when Mom and Dad and his sisters had gone their way, he walked past his Sunday school classroom and out the back door to the woods and creek across the street. He explored the path, the water, and the trees and thought it was the most amazing place to be. Losing track of time, he hurried back to church brushing off his shoes and pants.

Years later God would entrust to his care a wonderful family of his own, great friends, hundreds of thousands of acres, millions of beautiful trees and creeks, and a spirit to hear Him say, "This is the way, walk in it" (Isaiah 30:21). And day by day he learned each was a blessing and a calling from God.

His mom and dad are with the Lord now. The boy is as close as ever to his sisters and Jesus. Mom's prayers for her children were answered. They all love to honor and serve the Lord. The boy is thankful to know Mom and Dad still worship and serve Jesus, too, with all the hosts of heaven.

And now he understands why Mom was joyful that Sunday morning so long ago. A day is coming, by the grace of God, when we will all be together in church, again. Thanks, Mom! Thanks, Dad!

Preface

S acred stewardships are entrusted to us from God. Caring for them makes every day experiences a privilege and a joy—the people and resources we connect with a blessing—and God's calling, the yearning of our heart.

Unlike something we own, stewardships are not a possession. They are a trusteeship we serve for a time in accordance with God's will. The distinction between ownership and stewardship is not always clear in practice or perception. Many owners of vast resources have genuine hearts of trusteeship, while some trustees are unaware of the extraordinary stewardship in their care. Wherever we are on this spectrum, everyone is a trustee of something God has provided. There are no exceptions.

Sacred stewardships vary widely in form and function. Some examples include: a family farm, a corporate factory, a classroom, a boardroom, a volunteer job, an elective office, an hour of worship, a lifelong ministry, a neighborhood store, a global business, a performing art, an athletic talent, an office cubical, a verdant forest, a movie set, a music studio, a confidential meeting, a comment on social media, a commitment, a fulfillment, a friend, a prayer—and every thought, word, deed and day in our care.

Foundational to their well-being is our response to God's call and the motive of our heart. For it is God at work in every heart obedient to Him that makes a stewardship sacred.

All sacred stewardships have meaning and purpose beyond what we know or can imagine. With this in mind, there is no calling that is small or mountain too tall when we thankfully, humbly, and faithfully serve *for the love of Christ Jesus*.

William Linn Rutherford

CONTENTS

Chapter 1

Give Me Service

W hat does the phrase, *give me service* bring to mind? The context in which it is used may influence the answer, but so too will our preferences, habits, and goals. Interpretation of the phrase hinges on how we see ourselves in relation to its key actions: give and serve. If the preference is to be served, then we are the focus of someone else. If the priority is to give, then *someone else is our focus.*

"Give me service" can be thought of as a request and a goal. The word *me* connects the request *give* to the goal of *service.* That makes us a conduit of rendering service, not its destination. For some of us, the very idea of a life of servitude is offensive, repressive, and demeaning. Regardless of our comfort level with it, whether we know it or not, we all serve someone or something.

The question is not *if* we serve but *who* we serve and *why?*

The military is a great example. Women and men invest years and great effort defending their country. They deploy on a moment's notice from their home, loved ones, and community. They engage enemies, domestic and foreign, at great personal risks. They deal with untold hardships, suffering, and sacrifice.

Missionary work is another example. Men and women from all walks of life serve the Great Commission by sharing and living the Gospel and by providing hope, help, and care to people throughout the world. The challenges they face are great.

We may identify best with moms and dads. Parents are champions for their children. Their mission is every hour, day, and year. Nothing is too daunting for their help and prayers. Their body, soul and mind are devoted and spent for their child's protection and care. Parents are the mirror and model children see on their way to becoming the person they are going to be.

There are so many other examples of giving and service that impact our lives. A sick child inspires immeasurable love among people brought together in mutual care. Like no one before or since, this precious child gives profound blessings to every person they touch. Love like theirs is a gift that lasts forever, even when we are separated from them for a while.

A middle-aged man is released from jail on a winter night with nothing in his pockets and nowhere to go. Hitchhiking to the city, he is given a ride by people on their way to an AA meeting, which is help he happens to need. They ask if he would like to go. There he meets an exceptional woman who works at a local hotel. Shelter and provisions are generously provided. Within a day he is on the streets, giving warm winter socks away to homeless men and women he meets.

A remarkable woman rode public buses in the 1950s and '60s from Detroit to the suburbs every week, often with solitary walks to and from her destinations. She cleaned homes with exceptional care and kindness, but her true calling, embodied by a heart that shattered cultural barriers, was creating loving relationships. To her joy, her beloved children, a daughter and son, grew up to serve people through medicine and law enforcement. The influence of her presence and prayers, shared everywhere she worked, blessed many other children, too.

What is it about the military, missionaries, moms and dads, a child, a freed inmate, and a woman who loved uncondition-ally that inspires such service? If we were able to ask what motivated them, what might they say? Perhaps they would say love of country, love of humanity, love of family, and love which was given first to them. The answers are much alike. Their foundation is love, the focus is outward, and the func-tion is care.

Sacred stewardships are gifts from God that allow us the privi-lege of caring for someone or something in a way that produces an abiding love from Christ Jesus, through us to people we are blessed to know.

One way to discern sacred from secular is if our pride shows up. Sacredness seeks God's guidance in prayer, relying on His power, obeying His Word, trusting His will, and *giving Him glory*. Sounds easy for someone who loves the Lord—so what is the problem?

Think of the conduit in the phrase *give me service*. The problem is us. It is one thing to say, "God's will be done," and another to keep ours at bay. Our will, our way, and our pride often belie any sense of serving a sacred stewardship. Has anyone ever thoughtfully suggested a course of action different from your own, and your first thought was "I am in charge and will do as I see fit!" That may be your prerogative, but it confirms pride is in charge. When circumstances and self-interest drive our behavior, we replace the sacred *"Thy will be done"* (Matthew 6:10), with the secular, *my* will be done.

How do we keep our will out of the way? Keep God's Word every day for every need. Pray for women, men, and children on our mind, and for wisdom, discernment, and capacity to serve and fulfill God's plan. Seek opportunities to encourage, guide, and support people and resources temporarily in our care. Apply the humility George McDonald described as, "Humility is not thinking less of yourself—it's thinking of yourself less." Thanking God for all He does, trusting His will, and glorifying His name helps, too.

Think of the person we value above all others. Our desire is to be in their presence and to help them in every way we can. When they are away, we talk with them frequently. They are never far from our thoughts. We anticipate their return and are filled with joy when we are together again. These are hallmarks of someone we love and willingly serve. That is the way God sees us.

Do we long for His presence as much as He does for ours? Do we seek to be in His company and service? Do we experience joy in His glorification? These questions are fundamental to serving sacred stewardships.

First comes listening for, recognizing and responding to His call. It may be a long-term yearning of the heart. It may be a brand-new awakening that stirs our spirit. It may be an interest kindled by something we are doing right now. Sacred callings may also be discovered by showing up and being involved. Perhaps it is to serve a person or persons for whom we feel a deep conviction, or a cause or natural resource we are inspired to protect and serve. Sacred calls are uniquely suited to the one to whom it is entrusted, and their purpose is *always someone or something other than self*.

Consider Christ Jesus. After forty days of fasting, He did not succumb to temptations to put Himself first. Later, in an act of mercy, He fed thousands with a few fish and a little bread. From the cross, He could have summoned legions of angels to His aid, but that was not His purpose or prayer.

So, if yearnings of our heart or what stirs our soul is motivated by our prestige, prosperity or power it is likely not a calling to sacred stewardship. *To be sacred it will seek to serve and shine light on the sacrificial love of Christ Jesus.* It will be achieved not by us or even for us, but through us for the glory of God through Christ Jesus.

This is not criticism of ambition, success, or wealth. On the contrary, these are great blessings we welcome to use for His good. Rather, the desire is for each of us to recognize the source and goal of our sacred stewardship. But if they become about self, we are off track. *Returning to God's Word and the pattern of His life will restore the purpose of what He places in our care.*

Sacred stewardships render service in good and bad circumstances alike. Jesus embodied this. He did not return evil for evil. He did just the opposite. Those who opposed Him tried to discredit and bring charges of sedition against Him by asking whether taxes should be paid to Rome. Jesus replied, "Render to Caesar the things that are Caesar's, and to God the things that are God's" (Mark 12:17). His counsel applies to far more than taxes and to Rome. It is about honoring leaders and obeying civil and biblical law, then and now.

How we respond to His direction, to honor those in leadership and to honor God, will influence how, or if, we respond to His call to sacred stewardship. Some responses may be superficial, begrudging, or unwilling. Or they may be enthusiastic with commitment and gratitude. The esteem we have for the source will impact our response, willingness, and effectiveness.

Recognizing the source of the call, its sacredness and stewardship's most essential characteristic, is vital to serving all that God entrusts to our care. It helps to recognize and respond to the call if we know who is calling. *If we know Christ Jesus, we will recognize His voice and His way.* For example, even in a crowded place with activity all around, when someone we know and love calls our name, we recognize their voice. Or, in a quiet moment at work or at rest, there is no difficulty recognizing and being drawn to someone we know who enters our thoughts. Likewise, we recognize the sight and manner of someone we know, even at a distance. Their voice may not be audible, but we respond and trust them just the same.

Recognition of the call's source, Christ Jesus, leads to understanding the call's sacredness. It is from Him, for Him, to Him, and with Him. Anything less confirms it is not of Him. Above every motive that enters our heart, to be inspired to sacredness is set apart by being consecrated and blessed by God. Our service may be ignored or unvalued by man, but praise of man is not the goal.

Stewardship is the defining characteristic and means to serve and fulfill a sacred calling. It involves being entrusted with something of great value that belongs to another. An example is a friend who entrusts their child's well-being to your care. Or perhaps you are the one entrusting your child to them. This is an extraordinary act of trust by the one to whom the child belongs, and to whom the child is given. Trust is foremost in the relationship. It involves giving and receiving. The cornerstone of stewardship is trusteeship. *Like a parent entrusting a precious child to another, we receive from God's precious creation stewardships He gives into our care.* We receive them with thanks and give all we can to serve their well-being for Him.

This is not a conditional or proof-based trust—it is unconditional and faith-based. *It is faith in, reliance on, and willing submission to the person who is both God and man: Christ Jesus.* We are in the Lord's service and are representing Him. That may seem obvious to believers, but what indications of its truth do people who may not know God see?

Consider for a moment some life experiences we have had starting with mom and dad, to kids and adults we knew growing up, schools and churches we attended, groups and teams we belonged to, and to current friends and colleagues with whom we share our lives and work. In various ways they all influence our point of view and are reflected in what we value and do. For instance, as employees, we champion our company and are happy when our customers are pleased.

With this view, how do we represent our family and friends and what we hold most dear to the world around us? Is our heart for them transparent or camouflaged? What evidence do we show forth that others may see the great value we place upon serving and honoring them? How do we feel when others support them or mistreat them?

The answers come from deep in our soul and determine how we represent God by what we do for the people and resources He entrusts to us. One way His Spirit shines through us is our everyday conduct. Our motive and purpose communicate our focus and what we believe. Does it seek to honor and serve someone else? If so, what would we say if asked to explain who we serve and why?

At some point in our walk with Christ Jesus the answer is clear: *all that matters most to Him matters most to us.* What grieves the Spirit of God, grieves ours as well. His joy becomes ours. It comes naturally, then, to love as He loves—to give as He gives, and to serve and honor Him. So, we rejoice with every brother and sister in Christ from every nation, tongue, and tribe. This conduct may not be widely understood by everyone whom we love and serve, but it is by our Lord.

It is one thing to seek and recognize our sacred stewardship and another to intentionally serve it for God's glory. That is easier said than done. After all, our culture places great value

7

on earthly praise and reward, less so on God's. It is inherent to our focus on the here and now. Not only can we succumb to this culture, we can become the culture.

Compare the temporal view with the eternal view, and the priority and outcome can change. From an eternal view, our best is yet to be—nothing we have now will compare to being in His glory. In fact, all that is in our grip, every bit of worldly status, influence, possessions, and resources, will slip through our fingers with our last breath. This perspective is captured by the phrase, "Soon another life will pass, only what's done for Christ will last." That is why "get it while you can" is not Christ-centered. It is an enigma to sacred stewardship. It is the difference between being the one served and being the servant.

Consider the lives of the rich man and Lazarus. During his life on earth, the rich man was served and comforted while Lazarus had no such privilege or experience. In eternity their experiences are reversed. This does not mean wealth in this world is poverty in the life to come, or that poverty now is wealth to come. It teaches that what we do with all that is entrusted to us matters. *Service is not optional—it is foundational.*

Who we choose to identify with and serve is optional. The person who occupies the throne of our heart is up to us. Maybe we choose ourselves, our spouse, our children, or a celebrity. Perhaps it is our employer, customers, or savings account. But it cannot be someone or something else, plus God. Sooner or later one becomes secondary. God is foremost in our life, or He is not. The choice is ours. It is the most important choice we will ever make.

Give me service from the perspective of sacred stewardship is life's greatest purpose and joy. It is an opportunity to be in God's service for His glory. It confirms who is enthroned in our heart and who we represent and serve. It inspires, renews, and provides eternal meaning to life's daily duties. By God's grace, it is an answer to prayer that by His presence and power, our faith not only serves Him but may move mountains through Him.

With this point of view comes a confession. It is only by God's grace, power, and presence, and for His glory, not ours, that our faith and works can move mountains. We are neither the agent nor the object of its outcome. We are the ones seeking to serve, not the ones seeking to be served. Apart from Him our work does not glorify Him. If our goal is for our glory and praise, *it is time to check who we have enthroned in our heart.*

The thought of being called by Christ Jesus to bring glory to Him may seem unnecessary. After all, the glory of His creation is plain to see in the span and beauty of the earth, sea, and sky. The breath of life in every woman, man, child, and living thing testifies to His glory. How could the Author and Sustainer of all creation be glorified by anything we do? For others, the thought of being called by God to bring Him glory may seem far too difficult a task. We may feel self-conscious about publicly glorifying Him. Besides, there are people doing this already. What more can we add?

The answer to both questions is the same. Glory abounds to Christ Jesus through all we do *in His name.*

Yet, when we go through our day without a thought of Him, without gratitude for Him, without embodying His Spirit to people and resources entrusted to our care, and without a desire to honor Him through the life He has blessed us to live and share, then neither our heart nor the fruit of our labor will abound to His glory.

A desire to glorify Him is a good place to begin, but we may be tempted to think His calling is beyond our capacity to fulfill.

Or, we may believe no one will listen to us or act upon what we say or do. We may conclude there will be opposition, criticism, and consequences for living for Christ Jesus, instead of fitting into the times we live and seeking the approval of women and men. All of this may be true, but one thing is certain: it is not our strength or our will that will carry the day. God's calling is done *through* us not *by* us. It is His will that will be done. Examples of this are throughout the Bible: Abraham, Moses, Joseph, David, Gideon, Nehemiah, Ruth, and Esther to name a few.

Another point to consider is our ability to distinguish between a call from Christ Jesus and someone else. One way is by referring to God's Word, especially the Gospels of Matthew, Mark, Luke, and John. If the calling on our heart contradicts or adds to the Gospel of Jesus' life, His redemptive work, His sacrificial love, and forgiveness of sin, it is not a calling from God. Jesus said, "Because I live, you will live also" (John 14:19). So, before proceeding we must confirm our calling serves and glorifies His life—because He lives.

We should be cautious about anything we may hear, perceive, or be lead to follow that makes us the object and beneficiary of our call. Recall Jesus said that His Kingdom is not of this world. In other words, He is King with all the sovereignty, glory, honor, and power that entails. Yet, He laid it down to serve us: though He had no place to lay His head. He borrowed a donkey to enter Jerusalem. The Last Supper was in someone else's home. The Garden of Gethsemane belonged to another, and so did the tomb from which He rose to life again. As Creator and Redeemer of the universe, He could have claimed all He wished that was rightly His. *Instead He served and sacrificed so we may receive, through faith in Him, "what no eye has seen nor the heart of man conceived" (1 Corinthians 2:9).*

There is good reason to question the source and motive of a call that glorifies self. Jesus demonstrated self-control, not self-indulgence. If our stewardship is from Him, it will exalt Him. It will reflect His love, through us, to people and resources in our care, and it will lay up treasures in Heaven.

God's Word encourages us not to grow weary. This implies at times, we will be tested, we will struggle, we will not win, and we may not even see the fruit of our labor. But the One we exalt, Christ Jesus, will bring to fruition all we do for Him and much more.

So then, it follows that "give me service" in the context of sacred stewardship can be thought of as a brief and fervent prayer. It intentionally seeks opportunity and privilege to be in the Lord's presence, His service, and His power, provision, and promise. There may be similar aspirations we have to be in the presence of people we love or admire, or for jobs we seek and goals we strive to achieve, but what sets the prayer to serve Jesus apart from other hopes is who it seeks to glorify. It is not self or family. It is not employers, colleagues, or customers. It is not political affiliations or religions. It is Christ Jesus and the value we place on our relationship with Him.

A sacred stewardship is not a request our Lord makes pending our approval and acceptance. It is a trusteeship He places into our care. We are trusted not because we have earned it, but because it is given to us by Christ Jesus. What we do next, and what becomes of our stewardship, reflects who we choose to serve.

Chapter 2

Submission

Have you ever laid something down voluntarily of great value, something with which you did not want to part? There are many reasons people do this every day. Often after seeking God's direction in prayer, the decision is made to lay it down and move on. But letting go of something of great meaning can result in great heartache. Leaving it behind and walking away is not easy to do, especially when in submission to someone else's will.

Submission is a concept from which some of us recoil. It may be viewed as weakness, passivity, fearfulness, or a lack of confidence and ability. The great second baseman of the Brooklyn Dodgers, Jackie Robinson, who became a major league baseball player in 1947, submitted himself to the will of another, but it was not because of weakness, fear, or lack of ability. In fact, his valor, honor, strength of character, and skill soared above the culture of his time, and it still does.

We may never be called to do what Jackie Robinson did because there are very few with a heart like his, but *we will be called to choose who we submit to and why.* Jackie Robinson's choice was reflected by his great power under control, his vision to see beyond the headlines and hostilities of the day, and his determination to lift others up by his willing sacrifice to lay down something he valued. Intentional love like this, despite vile remarks hurled at him, is the Spirit of Christ Jesus who Jackie faithfully served.

Our life and actions reflect who we submit to, as well. Yes, we all are submissive, even those of us who abhor the thought. Whether to a life style, an ethnic heritage, a cause, political view, sports team, career, investments, or icons, *we all line up behind someone or something.* It is who and what we lift up, stand with, follow, and believe. Our choice is evident by what we do.

If our choice is Christ Jesus, something about us will reflect Him. He does not revile when reviled. He does not protest or shout in the streets. He creates and values everyone's life from conception through eternity. He sustains earth, space, and time, yet knows each of our names. He rejoices with all of His creation whenever someone chooses to trust and commit to Him. He weeps with all who do not. He embodies patience, reconciliation, mercy, grace, forgiveness, justice, and love.

Submission to Him will show forth His Spirit in some way by the choices we make. We cannot help but manifest the heart and vision of who we seek to spend our time with, commit our support to, and serve. If we are genuine, it will show up in some manner and time. It certainly did in Jackie Robinson, whose remarkable courage and restraint in the midst of unconscionable rejection and hate mirrored the power and passion of Christ Jesus.

Submission and obedience are two sides of the same coin. Seeing a steady red traffic light and coming to a complete stop is obedience. Slowing down, but proceeding across the intersection against the steady red, is not obedience. What we do, especially when no one is watching, says a lot about our inclination to obey.

We all have experience choosing between obeying and disobeying, honesty and dishonesty. Even as children, we stretched and broke some of mom and dad's rules, which they made for our safety and well-being. It is possible our first lie was in response to mom's question, "Did you eat the last of the cookies?" Instinctively seeking innocence, our reply may have been, "I'm not sure" or "I don't know" when the crumbs of the last bites were still on our chin. With practice and age, disobedience and lying become commonplace. We may even forget or devalue the purpose of honesty and the benefit of obeying rules: our safety and well-being. It takes a strong person to obey a code of conduct in all kinds of circumstances, especially when it is easier to go along so we fit in the group.

When Israel was captured by King Nebuchadnezzar of Babylon in 605 BC, Daniel was a teenager among thousands of Israelites taken captive. He and his three friends were selected for service to the king. The custom was for servants to eat the same rich food members of the king's royal court were served, but Daniel and his friends' diet followed Mosaic Law. He and his companion's risked punishment by asking permission to forgo the king's food in favor of the fruits and vegetables their diet allowed. Why would they do that? Why not just go along?

This is the same Daniel who by the power of God interpreted dreams for kings, and oversaw the king's counselors and magi, whose descendants many years later crossed a desert to Bethlehem to seek, find, and worship the Christ child prophesied in the Torah. Daniel also survived a night in the lion's den rather than cease worshiping God. His friends Hananiah, Mishael, and Azariah were equally obedient to God. They would not bow and worship the image of gold King Nebuchadnezzar had made, so they were thrown into the fiery furnace. The king said, "Did we not cast three men bound into the fire? But I see four loose, walking in the midst of the fire, and they are not hurt, and the appearance of the fourth is like a son of the god's" (Daniel 3:24-25).

Daniel and his friends, by God's providence, willingly served kings who governed the people, but *they were unwilling to compromise their conduct and obedience to God.*

There were great cultural, religious, and political objections to Daniel and his friends—and to Jackie Robinson. We know only a little of what their submission and obedience to God cost them, but it is enough to marvel at their great courage and the high price they paid through every evil they endured and overcame. On that day, when we are together with them and hear their testimony firsthand, then we will fully know the sacredness of the stewardship God entrusted to them, and how their *obedience and sacrifice forever glorifies God.*

The concept of sacrifice can be unsettling particularly when submission and obedience are included. Reasons vary, but one aspect that applies is sacrifice without personal cost is not really sacrificial. An example of this is when King David of Israel was told to create an altar to God for a sin David had committed. The owner of the site designated for the altar, Araunah, offered the property to the king for free, but David replied, "I will buy it. *I will not offer a sacrifice to God that cost me nothing*" (2 Samuel 24:24). In the same way, the service and sacrifice of Jackie Robinson, Daniel, and his friends was personal and costly. In our day, such a point of view may seem out of date and contrary to the way of the world. After all, David was a king and could afford it. The point is not our personal means, but like Jackie Robinson and Daniel, it is about the capacity and character of our heart. A reminder of how God sees sacrifice may help.

Consider the widow from the town of Zarephath during the time of the prophet Elijah. There was great famine in the land for it had not rained for years. The prophet saw this remarkable woman while she was gathering sticks to prepare a fire. He sought some water and bread from her for he was in need. She replied, "I have nothing baked, and only have a handful of flour and a little oil, and now I am gathering sticks that I may go in and bake it for me and my son" (1 Kings 17:12). This was to be their last meal for they had nothing left to sustain their lives. Elijah said, "Fear not, go and do as you have said; but first make me a little cake of it and bring it to me, and afterward make for yourself and your son. The jar of flour shall not be spent and the oil shall not fail, until the day the Lord sends rain upon the earth" (1 Kings 17:14). So she gave the last of her flour and oil to make a small cake of bread for Elijah. Her submission and sacrifice may not have been valued or even noticed by people of her time, but God noticed and we still do. Her flour and oil remained and provided for her household until the rains came again.

The value and application of our sacrifice is connected to the one to whom we submit. A question to ask and answer is, "Who do I submit to and serve above all?" Most answers can be grouped into one of the following broad categories: (1) me and mine—(2) others and theirs—or (3) God and His. For those who say "no one," please try again. Everyone submits to someone. For responses that include "all three and more," please try again—there can be only one above all others.

Answers to this question also shed light on our focus and the fruit of our labor. Focus on me and mine is inward: the glory is mine. Focus on others is outward: they are lifted up. Focus on God is upward: He is glorified. Distinguishing one from the other helps, but it is not the primary reason for asking the question.

Identifying our personal priority and purpose is the goal. Figuring this out provides clarity about the path we are on, who we are following, and the meaning of our life. Is it temporal or eternal? Our answer will also shed light on our relationship with Christ Jesus and the value we place on serving Him now and in His coming kingdom. If it is not our focus and joy now, it is unlikely to be in the life to come.

We can change. None of us stay the same. Throughout our lives and all the circumstances we experience and respond to, *our views and understanding change*. At some point, we may be self-absorbed. Other times, we may be captured by the culture or pressures of the day. There will come a time when we evaluate what we have done, what we are doing, and what we may yet do for the glory of Christ Jesus.

Outcomes reflect our growth and change and who we submit to and obey. The fruit of it may not be apparent to us now or to those who may mock or ridicule what we do, but when we obey and serve Jesus, we can take to heart what the prophet Elijah said: "Fear not." Our sovereign Lord sees and knows the cost of every sacrifice and what is real and honoring to Him. It is important we know, too.

Years ago, during a professional baseball game in Los Angeles, California, two people ran onto the field with an American flag. Their intent was to burn the flag. They failed, thanks to Rick Monday, the center fielder of the Chicago Cubs. Rick ran to where the two were crouched down with lighter fluid and matches in hand. His athletic skill clearly evident, he reached the flag in full stride before it was harmed and carried it to safety. Employees operating the stadium scoreboard expressed what many people in the ballpark and many others watching on television felt. The scoreboard read, "Rick Monday—You made a great play." Yes, he did.

Times have changed. For some of us, treating a country's national symbol with respect has, too. On a spring day in Los Angeles, more than forty years ago, a baseball player's heart, devotion, and humble service were on display. Grieved by the immanent desecration of his country's flag, he instinctively, without premeditation or plan, honored it in a moment that has transcended time. There was no mistaking Rick Monday's love for country. He sprinted to intervene. He acted decisively. There was no equivocation. Everyone knew where he stood.

Is our allegiance and devotion as clear? Does anyone in our circle know it is Christ Jesus we serve? Do we obey His Word to honor those in positions of authority and to lift up people who are in need? How do we reflect His heart to people He has blessed us to know? When do we instinctively run to honor Him? Is our heart grieved by what grieves His?

Being made in His image is to be created by His hand for His purpose. The Bible teaches God knit us together in our mother's womb. He is the Author of us all from the unborn and unseen to the most iconic and powerful. The prophet Ezra said, "Thou art the Lord, thou alone; thou hast made heaven, the heaven of heavens, with all their host, the earth and all that is on it, the seas and all that is in them, and thou preservest all of them; and the host of heaven worships thee" (Nehemiah 9:6). *All of life is sacred to Jesus.* So much so that He gave His life, so we may live forever with Him. His great love is for all of humanity and for saving individual lives.

In the book of Jeremiah, the prophet shared God was grieved by people's failure to listen to Him and to respond when He called. Many of us may have some experience not listening to someone or failing to respond to their call. Or perhaps we were the one ignored and not given a response. It grieves the heart, particularly when it is a loved one, a friend, or group of people we have served.

Imagine how the Creator, Sustainer and Redeemer of life, Christ Jesus, feels to be ignored or worse. It is one thing to be ignored and another to be absent from our thoughts, removed from our decisions and actions, and to be replaced in our hearts. Each bear witness to where we stand, and with whom we stand. *God's Word repeatedly reminds us not to be deceived.* If we are not grieved by what grieves the Spirit of God, if we are not listening to His Word and responding to His call, if we are not longing to be in His presence, and if we are not reflecting His light and love in choices we make, then there is reason to evaluate whose word and way we are following.

One way to consider this is from the context of how we use the precious time we are blessed with, the activities we most enjoy, and the message and tone of what we choose to read, watch, listen to, and repeat. What we think and how we react, who and what we identify with, who we answer to, and what we embody, teach, and speak is evidence of who we submit to and obey. It also conveys, intentionally or not, our faith and perspective on the origin, purpose, and destination of life.

Indications that Christ Jesus may be our focus is evident in many ways. A few include:

- Being sorrowful when He is dishonored

- Yearning to spend time with Him

- Reliance and faith in Him

- Trusting all to Him

- Celebrating communion in remembrance of Him

- Eagerly anticipating and awaiting His return

- Identifying and sharing spiritual gifts given to our care

- Serving and protecting people and resources He trusts to us

- Enjoying gatherings—small and large—with all believers in praise and worship of Him

- Public identification with Him in baptism

- Reverent thanks and awe for all His creation

- Spending daily time in Scripture

- Exercising spiritual disciplines

- Lifting the church and others up in intercessory prayer

- Reflecting and sharing His heart

- Hating what He hates, loving what He loves, and defending what He defends

- Obeying His commands

- Seeking opportunity to serve and glorify Him

- Willingness and availability to witness to the gift of His saving grace

This does not mean all who submit to Christ Jesus become Billy Graham–like. Though a call to global evangelism is extraordinary and a great blessing, so, too, is a call to shine our Savior's light and love wherever we are and in whatever way we can. For stay-at-home moms or dads, it may be caring for the precious child who looks to you for help, protection, and guidance. For public employees, it may be to sacrifice for and serve people and resources with which you have been entrusted. For a health-care provider, it may be to know that Jesus is the Creator and Savior of life. For a salesperson, it may be the warm welcome and assistance you offer a customer, a reflection of God's heart in you. For educators, perhaps it is awakening and encouraging God-given talents with which your students have been endowed and in so doing co-laboring in the work of God. For a scientist, your mind of inquiry and spirit of truth may humbly explore and explain phenomena miraculous in design and function. From the words we use to the attitude we share, the beliefs we hold, and the motive behind what we do, it is all an opportunity, wherever we are and whatever we do, to witness by our words and deeds the glory of God.

Each of us is enabled to serve everything God entrusts to our care. We have an important purpose to fulfill, but first is the decision to intentionally submit to His will. Christ Jesus knows our purpose for He alone is the Author and Redeemer of our life. But there are times we go our own way with minimal desire for Him or thought about His involvement in our day. When this is the case, we should not anticipate knowing, let alone fulfilling His purpose for our life. We cannot live apart from Him and know and fulfill His will. Upon committing to and answering His call, *we learn and serve and are prepared for additional sacred stewardships* He places in our care. Each may be different than the one before, as we are different than we were before. Best of all, we get to know Him better by being in His presence daily.

There are many good people who passionately believe our thoughts shape our lives and the destiny of the world. As important as our thoughts are, this point of view seems to mis-understand or disbelieve the sovereignty of God. Our thoughts are vital and influence our lives in many ways and the lives of our brothers and sisters around the world—but only God cre-ates life, restores life, and can save the world.

Neither our thoughts nor power can bring into being all that is and ever will be. Our thoughts are powerless to make a new dawn every twenty-four hours or to make the moon orbit about the earth, impacting the oceans tides and the world's environment. Our thoughts cannot guide the earth around the sun every twelve months at precisely the right distance to allow the planet to be inhabitable. There is no personal power of our thought that can raise to new life someone who is without Christ. God's Word teaches, "They do not regard the deeds of the Lord, or see the work of His hands" (Isaiah 5:12). If we do not hold the deeds of Deity in high regard, and we do not see the work of His mighty hands, how can we ascribe to ourselves the power to save the world?

It is by God's power we are created, and by His provisions we live. It is by His mercy and grace we are sustained, and by His atonement for a fallen world we are redeemed. In the absence of reverence, gratitude, and love for Him, we fall victim to substituting our power for His and may choose to worship creation instead of the Creator. King David's question, "How long shall my honor suffer shame?" (Psalm 4:2) addressed the rebellion of his son, Absalom, but it also mirrors our regard for and submission to God. As the question applies to God, perhaps the answer is until we fully trust and submit to His sovereignty and power to deliver all of His creation in accordance with His purpose and plan.

Submission is perhaps the most valuable gift we can give to another. It is a sacrifice with real cost and consequence and confirms it is God who is in control. God has given us free will. The choice of whom or what we submit to is ours. It is the choice that impacts life now and life to come. It is one we should share with our loved ones, for Christ Jesus already knows if we have or will accept His invitation when He said, "Come to me, all who labor and are heavy laden, and I will give you rest. Take my yoke upon you and learn from me—for I am gentle and lowly in heart, and you will find rest for your souls. For my yoke is easy, and my burden is light" (Matthew 11:28-30).

To follow Christ Jesus is to live for His glory. This is demonstrated by our trust and worship of Him, sharing Him with others, recognizing His nearness and blessings, having remorse for failing Him, and rejoicing in the forgiveness He supplies. Being faithful to Him is not a partial commitment or picking and choosing what we like and discarding or rationalizing the rest.

It is fully surrendering our will, our way, and our life to His will, His way, His life, and His kingdom. This is not weakness, nor is it loss. In fact, what we see is enormous strength and uncompromising determination and great victory in men like Jackie Robinson and the prophet Daniel. For the one we submit to (and we all submit to someone) is the one whose strength, spirit, and victory we embody and share.

Not knowing this, but searching after it, is a hopeful sign, but not caring about it or disbelieving it is a warning sign. In both cases we become part of someone, and our *submission becomes integral to our spirit and life.* Submission to Christ Jesus affirms that we entrust to Him the well-being of all that He entrusts to us.

Chapter 3

We All Teach

There is a proverb that teaches, "I give you good precepts: do not forsake my teaching" (Proverbs 4:2). We are all teachers. We teach our family, our circle of friends, those we work with and for, acquaintances we meet briefly, and others we may never meet but reach through other means, such as someone we had contact with who shares something we said or did. Likewise, as we engage with one another, we receive, for each person we meet is a teacher, too.

What do we teach and to what end?

We teach many things including our priorities, what motivates us, what we believe, what we strive for, who and what we identify with, what we honor and love, and what we are willing or unwilling to compromise. Depending on our conviction for each one and our mode of engaging with others, we may even teach enmity by intent or default with people and opinions whose perspectives differ from our own. We teach these things, and many more *by the life we live and the choices we make*, by what we say and how we say it, by what we do and how we do it, by our attitudes and reactions to circumstances and people, by what we stand for, and by how we serve our sacred stewardship.

The possible outcomes of what we teach are wide-ranging. People may be ennobled or marginalized, inspired or discouraged, and their dreams may be supported or obstructed. We may foster hopefulness or despair by perpetuating a cycle that ends poorly for them or by sharing one that opens a new vision and blessings they did not have before. Other outcomes of our teaching may be short term and task oriented while some may be long term and strategic. The way we interact and teach can set the tone for our relationships and convey gratitude for every person who is a part of our life and family whether at home, work, school, church, or play. It is up to them, though, to choose if they want to be a part of our life.

There is a saying that *God has no grandchildren,* only children. No one becomes a member of the family of Christ Jesus because they are related to someone who is. To be in His family is a choice we make, individually, by faith in Him. God the Father and God the Holy Spirit bring us to Jesus, God the Son, but it is only by our free will that we let Jesus into our life and give Him Lordship over who we are and all we do. When we open the door and receive Him, we become a member of His family and are changed forever. The yearning of His heart becomes the yearning of ours. His steadfast love and righteousness become far more valuable than all our worldly affections and possessions.

Christ Jesus said, "Every sin and blasphemy will be forgiven men, but the blasphemy against the Spirit will not be forgiven" (Matthew 12:31). This reflects our Savior's authority, mercy, and judgment. We learn from the Bible that heaven rejoiced over His creation of the world; that the prodigal son's return was celebrated by his father—the tax collector who prayed, "God, be merciful to me a sinner!" (Luke 18:13) was justified; what Joseph's brothers meant for evil was used by God for good—that heaven and hell are real, and that our life, memories, and self-awareness are eternal. To deny, mock, or blaspheme the Spirit of God, is to dishonor or give credit to someone or something else for His miracles, blessings, and our salvation. To overlook or attribute these to anything other than the love and glory of God is to ignore a precept the Bible makes clear: "At the name of Jesus *every knee should bow, in heaven and on earth and under the earth, and every tongue confess that Jesus Christ is Lord, to the glory of God the Father"* (Philippians 2:10-11).

There is so much in life we diligently plan for, anticipate and do from our earliest days in school, to part-time jobs, housing, career, marriage, family, health care, community service, elections, investments, retirement, recreation, and even the food we eat. *Anticipating our eternal home warrants attention*, too, and it is reflected through how we share and teach sacred stewardships in our care.

Christ Jesus took our place, suffered the penalty for our sins, died, and rose again. He met with and commissioned His disciples and gave assurance He would always be with them and us. He ascended to heaven where He is interceding for our good. He is awaiting the day and hour of His return. Our faith in Him secures our salvation. There is nothing we do to earn it, buy it, or deserve it. If there were another way to be saved, the Word of God, Christ Jesus, would not have become flesh, dwelt among us and manifested His glory and atonement for us on the cross. To know we are loved changes us. To know we are loved like this saves us.

So we look forward to resurrection life and communion like never before, with the sufferings of Christ Jesus, and that moment we behold, for the first time, His face and the glory of Heaven.

Awestruck wonder awaits, as we discover the perfect holiness, power, justice, mercy, grace, and redemptive plan of our Father, Savior, and Holy Spirit. The host of heaven will be singing for joy. We will be overcome by meeting face to face and talking with Christ Jesus. "There is no condemnation for those who are in Christ Jesus," (Romans 8:1) but with sorrow we may see and understand what we failed to do with the many blessings and sacred stewardships entrusted to us. All darkness will be gone in that eternal day. There will be unimaginable joy and freedom from our sins and passion to join in the chorus of praise, worship, and glory to our Creator and Redeemer God. Absent will be pain, deterioration, suffering, separation, division, loss, and doubt. Beyond anything we have ever known, we will rejoice with tears of joy as we are reunited with loved ones, friends, and even foes with whom all differences are reconciled.

With counsel, anointing, and love, Christ Jesus will give us a new name. We will be enthusiastically engaged in work, learning and fulfilling His will, which will be ours, too, for His world and His family. With countless brothers and sisters in Christ, some we know and many others with whom we will become fast friends and with whom we will surely rejoice, we will give eternal glory and thanks for our mighty Savior's sacrifice, resurrection, and sovereignty over all creation and every life from the womb to heaven's majesty. Forever we will bear witness to His promise, "to make all things new" (Revelation 21:5).

The writer of the book of Hebrews stated, "For though by this time you ought to be teachers, you need someone to teach you again the first principles of God's Word" (Hebrews 5:12). The meaning of this precept is clear: *we have a responsibility to teach*. It also indicates our tendency to forget or forsake what we have learned. It makes unspecific reference to "someone" teaching again. Perhaps, it is the teacher we had at first, or someone else we know, or maybe someone we are yet to meet.

Let's assume it is one of us. How do we respond if teaching His precepts is what God has placed on our heart? Our first response is to give thanks and confirm God's direction and to understand how He has equipped and enabled us. We may not realize we are the right person for the job. This was true of Moses, Esther, and Ananias, the disciple who God chose to restore Saul's sight. Perhaps, we may be afraid of the powers aligned against us. This was the case with ten of the twelve who spied out the land of Canaan for the Israelites. There may be unimaginable problems, such as happened to Job, Jonah, Joseph, and David. Or, maybe, our spirit is expectant and determined like that of Noah, Mary, Ruth, and Nehemiah.

Whichever of these dispositions apply to us, we can take comfort in the knowledge that if it is truly God's calling, He has prepared us. He is present with us. He is for us no matter who opposes us. *He will triumph!* The problem comes when we forget or distort His precepts—fail to trust, rely, and call on Him—and choose to go our own way. It is ironic that when we do this, our reaction may be to blame God for leading us astray or abandoning us. How is this possible when we abandoned Him? That would be like blaming our mother or father, who do all they can to help us, for something we have done—or, taking credit for what we have been given and how we have been prepared and guided by so many people throughout our life. *Blaming, ingratitude, and the absence of joy are red flags* that the path we are on is our choosing, not God's.

When Christ Jesus was put to the test with the question, "Teacher, what shall I do to inherit eternal life?" Jesus replied, "What is written in the law? How do you read?" The questioner responded, "You shall love the Lord your God with all your heart, and with all your soul, and with all your strength, and with all your mind—and your neighbor as yourself." Jesus said, "You have answered right—do this and you will live." Then the man asked the genuine question on his heart, "And who is my neighbor?" (Luke 10:25-29)

In His answer, Christ Jesus shows us how to teach with mercy and love. The Lord knew the man's motive. His first question was not about seeking wisdom or guidance—rather, it was to test Jesus and to gain recognition for himself. Jesus was merciful and asked the man to recall what was written in the law—then the Lord confirmed that the man's answer was correct and admonished him to keep the precept he quoted. Christ Jesus taught by reminding him, and us, that answers to our questions are found in God's Word. He also revealed, by His love and direction, "Do this and you will live." There is more we need to learn and apply, like how to identify our neighbor and to share with her or him the mercy and grace embodied in our Lord.

Mercy is a remarkable gift illustrated by stories like the mother pleading for mercy for her son who had committed a crime, and being told, "Your son does not deserve mercy." She replied, "If it was deserved, it would not be mercy." Mercy is not receiving the punishment we deserve.

Grace is also an astounding gift represented by the expression, "*God's Riches at Christ's Expense.*" *The transaction that happened at Calvary's cross* exchanging our sins for the righteousness of Christ exemplifies it. Grace is receiving what we do not deserve.

Love is the greatest gift of all. Foundational to mercy, grace, and justice, love is the heart of the Gospel's good news and the essence of our Triune God's Spirit. "For God so loved the world that He gave His only Son that whoever believes in Him should not perish but have eternal life" (John 3:16). Christ Jesus came to save and free us from the penalty of our sins. His love gives all, forgives all, and saves all, and it resides in us by the Spirit of God. We may deny it or fail to give thanks for it, but we cannot live without it.

Love like this is pictured by a songbird caught in threads of plastic tangled around its leg and caught in the twig of a tree. Exhausted from trying to fly and free itself, held tight and trapped, it hangs upside down, dying, as other birds seem to call for help. Someone hears, sees, and reaches out, breaking the threads that bound the bird tight, even to death, and sets the bird free. Did the bird understand all that happened? Maybe, maybe not, but it certainly knew, it was bound, and now it is free.

Whether we have learned this about ourselves depends on our awareness and experience of the things we may be tangled in and the connections we have with each other and our teachers. Teaching has an outcome that is influenced by the connections we share. If the people we have interaction with matter to us, really matter, the outcome will be different then if they do not. If they care about us, the same is true—teaching will uplift, and the outcome will prove it.

On the road to Emmaus, two disciples of Jesus were discussing with despair His death and the apparent end of all hope that He was the one to redeem Israel. The Lord came alongside of them, though they did not know it was Jesus, and He asked them about the conversation they were having. Hearing their reply, Christ Jesus began to teach out of love for them, and for us, knowing the questions, doubts, fears and needs of their hearts. After the day was far spent, the two invited Jesus to take shelter and food with them for the night. It was *in breaking bread and giving thanks they recognized the Lord* before He vanished from their sight. They said to one another, "Did not our hearts burn within us as He talked with us on the road, while He opened to us the Scriptures?" (Luke 24:32)

Christ Jesus loved these men, and they loved Him. The outcome of their time together and His teaching transformed their hearts from sorrow to joy. Rushing back to Jerusalem that night, their hope restored and alive, they announced to the eleven and those who were with them that they had seen the risen Lord. How might their encounter with the Lord and the eleven have turned out in the absence of love? Perhaps, there would have been a lecture and some notes taken, or the dialogue may have included some humor, distractions, and questions—or maybe even a desire, knowing the lateness of the hour, to get on with other pressing issues. There is no need to speculate because there was love and learning. Their connection was impacted by the genuine care they had for one another.

This is true of our teachable moments as well. *If there is love, the potential for impact is far greater than if there is not.* Think of our family, who we love with all our heart, and who love us. They watch, listen, engage, and learn from all we say, do, and think.

Do we love others this way, with attention and care for each one? The degree to which we do, or do not, will impact everyone God blesses us to know, as will the presence or absence of their love for us. What about people who mistreat us? Do we love them?

As Christ Jesus was crucified, spikes driven through His sinless flesh and His cross lifted up, He prayed out loud, saying, "Father, forgive them—for they know not what they do" (Luke 23:34). Two men being crucified beside Him joined with the crowd in reviling the giver of life, the One who was dying to give them new life. One of them repented and, confessing Jesus as Lord, asked Jesus to remember him when He came into His Kingdom. Jesus replied, "Truly, I say to you, today you will be with me in Paradise" (Luke 23-43).

One of the Lord's closest friends, Simon Peter, who was filled with self-confidence and pride, said to Jesus and to all the apostles, "If I must die with you, I will not deny you" (Mark 14:31). Yet the night of Jesus' mock trial, Peter publicly, assertively, and repeatedly denied knowing his beloved Lord. Even so, after Jesus rose from the dead, He embraced and restored Peter, entrusting to him one of the greatest blessings and leadership privileges of all time: proclamation of the Gospel of Christ Jesus and stewardship of His church.

Do we forgive and lift up people who hurt us? Perhaps not like Christ Jesus, but by His Spirit abiding in us, we can. Wisdom for living in His Spirit is provided in a verse from the Book of Colossians. "As therefore you received Christ Jesus the Lord, so live in Him, rooted and built up in Him and established in the faith, just as you were taught, *abounding in thanksgiving*" (Colossians 2:6-7).

First, *receive Christ Jesus*. To receive Him is to believe and confess He is Lord and Savior. By doing so, our salvation in Him is settled and certain. Upon its receipt, "Who shall separate us from the love of Christ" (Romans 8:35). Believing and receiving is a voluntary act of our will. He does not force Himself into our heart. Nor is His gift of salvation contingent on our works or some imaginary scorecard of our life. Receiving Him changes our outlook, output, and outcome.

Second, *live in Him*. To live in Jesus is to know that our life is in Him. It is the relationship that provides our greatest motivation, joy, and peace. He is the one in whom our identity and reason for living reside and whose daily provisions care for us. Without Him in our life, our purpose, and our focus can wither and wane, but in His presence, we are refreshed and strengthened. To live in someone like this means they are never far from our thoughts, no matter where we are or what we do. *Our decisions and actions reflect the one for whom we live.* To live in Jesus is to reflect Him.

Rooted and built up in Him is a product of receiving Him and living in Him. This precept is reminiscent of God's glorious trees, whose stability and well-being are connected to the site in which their roots are anchored. Fundamental to the growth of trees is sunlight, soil, water, and air. Each is a provision they must receive, take in and use for their building up. However, it is not in themselves that these requirements are supplied, but by God's creative design and provisions. The presence, growth, and magnificence of trees exemplify being rooted and built up in Jesus—so it is with us. It is not something we do for ourselves, but what Christ Jesus does in us. He is the source and supplies all provisions we require. Our growth in Him is not our doing, but God's. Through us, His love is shared with people *we are blessed to be connected with by His providence.*

Established in the faith is an infinite and pure spring of water flowing through us from being rooted and built up in Christ. A prayer many of us may have prayed is, "Give me more faith." A similar prayer is the request of a man in Scripture, who said to Jesus, "I believe—help my unbelief" (Mark 9:24). These prayers confirm faith is given to us by God. It is not something we manufacture. It may become more effective, but not more abundant. The gift of faith is not metered out in proportion to our need or circumstance. It is given to all who believe in Christ Jesus, the source and fulfillment of our faith. If, or when, our faith falters, we can be certain this is not from God. For upon being established in faith, we do not receive more, nor is what we have taken away. We are established. It is done. *God is faithful. Our part is remaining faithful to Him.*

The reference in the verse to "just as you were taught" affirms we are students, benefitting from the teaching God provides. Sharing what we learn proves it matters to us, even more it proves the people we share it with matter to us.

So the question isn't that we teach—but who, what, how, and why we teach. Whether or not our loved ones, friends, circle of acquaintances, and people we may meet only briefly listen to or act upon what we share is out of our hands. Our responsibility is not what they do, but what we do in love for them. It is not to harass or condemn, but to love as we are loved by Jesus. So we teach in His Spirit the sacred stewardship entrusted to us by caring for each other, praying with and for each other, and forgiving each other just as we have been forgiven.

The Lord's disciples knew He prayed daily, and they asked Him to teach them to pray. The prayer God taught includes these words and condition of the heart: "Forgive us our debts, as we also have forgiven our debtors" (Matthew 6:12). We may confess our sins with these words or words like them. We may also fail to fulfill the second part of the prayer. Retaining animosity, bitterness, or grudges is the opposite of what our Lord taught us to pray and to be: people who forgive. These words confess our daily sins. For all of us sin and have fallen short of God's righteousness, and for this we seek His forgiveness, but we also seek to forgive the ones by whose hands we have suffered. To ask for one without giving the other is to deny them both.

We aspire to forgive as God does, but to be *abounding in thanksgiving,* which concludes the verse from Colossians, seems almost impossible. After all, there are days, circumstances, and people at odds with our ability to feel good about what is happening, let alone to have a heart that abounds in thanksgiving. It is not what is outside of us, but who is inside of us that inspires abounding gratitude. To abound is to overflow. It cannot be contained. People who abound with the gift of making music must make it. A person gifted in photography must capture the image they seek. Girls and boys gifted by God in infinite ways must follow their dreams. Abounding is an outward expression of an inner condition that reflects our deepest joys and passion.

To abound in thanksgiving is to overflow with gratitude for God. When things are going great, that may seem easy and even natural, but even then, when we are blessed with good health, prosperity, and security, our expressions of *thanksgiving may be tempered by prideful thinking,* believing these things are of our own making and are what we deserve. Plus, with the busy pace of our life and so many demands requiring our attention, unless we truly feel it and make it a personal priority, abounding in thanksgiving may not be a prevailing thought of our heart, let alone something we do.

What about times and situations when things are not so good, in fact when they are bad, are we to abound in gratitude for them? Not necessarily for the afflictions or suffering, but for what they produce. The love and support we receive, the insight and understanding we gain, and for the remarkable ways we can be changed. Christ Jesus said, "In the world you have tribulation: but be of good cheer, I have overcome the world" (John 16:33). So does everyone who places their trust in Him. If nothing else, suffering can awaken in us how helpless and hopeless we are to draw our next breath or for our heart to beat one more time, apart from the grace of God. These are good reasons for abounding in gratitude, but they need not be limited to our trials. Daily prayers we lift up for one another also abound in thanksgiving to God.

Other than cheering wholeheartedly for our favorite teams and celebrities, abounding is not something we normally do. It is more natural to be cautious about words we choose and the amount of enthusiasm we convey. Tailoring our words and joy to fit the people and places we are connected with is more customary than abounding with thanksgiving to God.

So, to love, forgive, and lift up people like Christ Jesus does, we receive Him, live in Him, are rooted and built up in Him, established in the faith, as we were taught, and we abound in thanksgiving in good and bad times. We do this because *we are His, and He is ours*.

We all teach. Scripture confirms God does, too. "Who is a teacher like Him?" (Job 36:22) Teaching is a great privilege and solemn responsibility. *What we teach and the motive of our heart can help or harm the people in our life*. For this reason, as teachers, we are held to a high standard of accountability, not only for its impact in this life and generation, but for generations and life to come. It has always been and will always be that teaching is not for ourselves, but for all we are blessed to connect with by God's providence and purpose.

Sharing only with people we are close to, or only what they want to hear is not teaching—it is ignoring or editing what God has instructed us to do. Thomas Jefferson, author of the Declaration of Independence and third president of the United States, deleted Scriptures from the Holy Bible he did not believe. Today there are some who follow his example. Others avoid or dispute the books of Genesis and Revelation. Some publicly mock and disdain God's Word. It may be for different reasons than President Jefferson's editing, but God's direction is clear: "teach them to observe all I have commanded you" (Matthew 28:20).

So, we are to teach as God leads us. It affirms what we have learned and who we serve. Like teachers before us who inspired and championed patterns of life, our teaching will also have a legacy. It will include our gratitude to Christ Jesus that by His Spirit in us we kept and shared and did not forsake His teaching. *By God's grace and Spirit, those we reach will teach, too.*

Chapter 4

One Day

The Holy Bible reveals the awesome power of our Creator God. God speaks about creation in chapters 38 through 42 of the book of Job. The Gospel of John identifies Jesus as the Creator of everything. The book of Genesis is a chronology of the beginning. Some dismiss these Scriptures as myth and superstition. Others believe parts of them, like heaven is real (also one of God's creative works), but are unable or unwilling to believe the rest. Whether we believe completely, in part, or not at all is our free will, another creation of our God.

Moses wrote, "In the beginning God created the heavens and the earth. The earth was without form and void, and darkness was upon the face of the deep—and the Spirit of God was moving over the face of the waters. And God said, 'Let there be light'—and there was light. And God saw the light was good—and God separated the light from the darkness. God called the light Day, and the darkness He called Night. And there was evening and there was morning, one day" (Genesis 1:1-5). The first manifestation of God's power, recorded in Genesis, is light. Yet, it was not until the fourth day that God created the sun. So, *there is something about this first light,* which made evening and morning and one day that is foundational to life.

Our calendars may provide some insight. A day is the time it takes the earth to rotate once around its northern axis. A month is the days it takes the moon to circle the earth. A year is the days required for earth to orbit the sun. A week is the days described in Genesis. Time is numbered by days. Something that may seem so commonplace, the rising and setting of the sun, is an amazing part of God's creation. One day followed by another is completely outside of our will or power to control or make happen, even once. Like a divine watch, the earth rotates at the right speed, angle and distance from the sun.

Farther away and the temperature of the earth would fall, closer it would rise. Slow the earth's rotational speed by one third, and the day would be seventy-two hours long, plunging the world into longer periods without sunlight. Imagine life, if life can be imagined or maintained, with such a foundational change to one day.

Scripture declares, *"This is the day which the Lord has made, let us rejoice in it and be glad"* (Psalm 118:24). Although this verse speaks about the day of our salvation, in which we will surely be rejoicing, it also captures the awesome wonder and great blessing of each new day. How we view and live this miracle depends on our frame of reference and expectations. For example, children unaware of their Creator and Sustainer God may not give the rising of the sun a moment of thought, other than the impact it may have on their play. For teens with years ahead to fulfill their dreams, their thoughts may understandably be on the future. Career-aged people are busy getting the job done. Those who have completed their employment years may have their sights set on fulfilling retirement plans. Yet, in every age group, children of God are thanking Him for the day. For some of us it may not be until an accident, injury, or passing of a loved one or the approach of our own mortality that we recognize each day for what it is: a gift from God.

We need not suffer injury to be inspired by, and grateful for, the days our Creator provides. His miraculous dawn is seen by people everywhere in the world. What a great reminder of His power and His daily care for our good. Not a single person is left out, nor is anyone higher than another. His light shines on everyone. But, if we take it for granted, then the rising and setting of the sun, whether glorious in splendor or covered by clouds, is little more than a natural phenomenon with no greater or less merit than yesterday's, today's, or the one we expect tomorrow.

However, our nearest star is a faithful and great provision God has made for our lives. It displays His providence and sovereignty and is seen in the intimate relationship between sunlight and trees. In the warm light of spring, blossoms and leaves appear, confirming renewal and restoration of life. In the radiant heat of summer, trees receive the sun's energy, yielding growth to their stature and capacity, year by year transforming seedlings into forests. With fall's shorter and cooler days, foliage may display an array of colors that were always there but unseen. Resilient, patient, and enduring through winter, trees rest, containing a storehouse of energy derived from the sun that by God's grace is drawn upon for their good and ours in days to come. *In all seasons of life, Jehovah Jireh, the Lord our Provider, is found.*

With this in mind, sunrise is far more than just another day. It is a gift and opportunity God provides. But, like all gifts, it is up to the recipient to choose what to do with it.

If we see our life and each day as a provision from God, we have a perspective of its source, purpose, and blessing. If we do not, then something else is on our mind about its source and purpose. Both points of view cannot be true. The one we hold frames the context of our day and life and our reason for being here.

With time comes change in perspective. Something we once liked may not be what we like today. Things we did years ago, we no longer do now. What we wanted once, we may not want anymore. What we value most today may not have been on our mind before. Time and experience change us. We can be limited or improved by it, based on our prayers, point of view, and their application in our lives.

We may conclude there is not enough time in the day to do all we want. We may decide the time required to accomplish a goal is just too much. Or, the timing of something that is on our heart is just not right. In contrast, the constraint of time may motivate action that was thought impossible. We may recognize there is no time like the present. Or the thought in our heart may take precedence over circumstances that tell us, "not now." Who we trust and turn to influences the choice we make and path we take, as will our understanding and care of time.

We consume time. It is not something we make, set aside, or replenish. Neither can it be redone or erased. But we can care for today. We can invest our time, we can share our time, we can value every day, and we can make our time count for the benefit of others. How we apply it reflects our motives and priorities.

Moses prayed, *"Teach us to number our days that we may get a heart of wisdom"* (Psalm 90:12). These are words to live by, because our days and the opportunities they hold for renewal, growth, and service are numbered. So, whether we are younger or older, every day at work, school, play, rest, and worship are precious. Wisdom that reflects this is not revealed in rushing about to experience as much as possible, but in slowing down enough to see and savor what may otherwise be a blur or taken for granted, like the blessing of one day and the remarkable people we get to meet and know.

Unconvinced of this truth, or unmoved by the sacredness of twenty-four hours, there may come a time, as our days turn to years and then to a lifetime, that we consider where and how we spent our time and what difference it made and to whom.

There may be sorrow over missed opportunities and squandered time, or there may be peace, fulfillment, and joy in the knowledge we served and treasured all that Christ Jesus temporarily gave to our care.

Years ago, a popular song entitled "Big Yellow Taxi," written and performed by Joni Mitchell, captured the sense of loss that can be realized after something is gone. The chorus reflects what many of us have experienced. "Don't it always seem to go that you don't know what you got 'til it's gone?"

As much as this thought applies to things and people we have loved and been separated from, it can be even more impactful to the precious gift of time that is given into our care and is passing through our hands. No matter who we are, regardless of age, creed, culture, and connections, none of us can make a day. Not for ourselves, not for loved ones, and not for anyone or anything else. There is a saying related to the value of land: "No one is making any more of it." The reasoning holds that as land becomes less available, its value increases. This applies to our time as well. As there is less of it, for countless reasons, its value may be appreciated and applied in ways it never was before.

We express this awareness in gratitude for someone or something. Not the kind we think of as the proper thing to do, like "Thank you for the present" or, "You did a really good job today" but the kind that is motivated from a genuine heart of affection for the person who gave the gift or who did the job. There is a big difference between the two. One lifts up *something,* the other lifts up *someone.* Both are valuable and kind, but only one focuses on the person, only one builds a deep foundation, and only one yields potential for growth.

Genuine affection for someone is accompanied by a heartfelt willingness and desire to stand with them. This is not a benevolent, philanthropic, altruistic, or even leadership condition of the heart—it is a deep-seeded part of who we are. It is by our connections and affection for one another that we see a glimpse of the love Christ Jesus has for us.

We suffer when others suffer. We rejoice when they rejoice. We remember, serve, love, and pray for each one. This is not a coincidence or happenstance of some evolutionary chain of random events—it is an endowment from the heart of our Savior to ours and reflects His great love for each of us. We are made in His image, which includes having His priorities. Throughout our life, we are given opportunities to share His abundant love with each other and with all of His creation. But, we have to grow our capacity to love like God, our Father, "Who did not spare His own Son but gave Him up for us all" (Romans 8:32). This is love that loved us before we loved Him. It is sacrificial, impartial, and faithful love. Nothing can separate us from this love.

We can love like this, too. Every time we see someone the way Christ Jesus does, every time we listen and do not condemn, every time we provide encouragement and help, every time we sacrifice ourselves, every time we face dread with peace and faith—every time we pray for and forgive one another, and every time we bless God. Some days we are better at it than others. When we see Christ Jesus in all creation, His unparalleled devotion and sacrifice for us, His daily presence and provisions in our life, and His saving grace, by faith alone, then we share His love. But if we forget the Source and Sustainer of the day, overlooking His blessings in each one, changing the good news of the Gospel, failing to give Him our thanks and praise, that day will not be one of our best sharing His love. It is what we reflect of Christ Jesus that reveals our relationship with Him and whether or not it is His calling, or another's that is on our heart. God already knows. It is one thing to talk a good game, to look the part, to do the right things, to be at all the right functions, and have people who believe in us—but *it is something altogether different for Jesus to be resident in our heart.*

When the winds of advancing storms come into our lives, what we expect and who we turn to reveals who is in our heart. There is no doubt that wind is a powerful force that can produce anxiety, damage, and even death, but above the dark and gathering clouds, there is clear sky and light without end.

Whether we focus on darkness or light, and which we choose to dedicate our energy and attention to will influence how we live. In the darkness of Gethsemane, Christ Jesus could have focused on the night and the severity of the approaching storm— He could have run for His life like His disciples did. Instead, the Son of God prayed to His Father and ours. Upon praying, "your will be done" (Luke 22:42) He rose in peace to meet the Roman cohort and the Sanhedrin's guard.

He was not focused on the storm or the suffering to follow, but on the light He knew was present and coming. It was not His life He was protecting that night but ours. He was in charge, not the mob. He demonstrated this in an act of divine love by restoring to wholeness a man whose ear Peter had just cut off. Scripture says Jesus touched the man's ear and healed him. It does not say Jesus picked up the severed ear from the ground, cleaned it off, and reattached it. He created an ear. Even *in the darkness of that solemn night, our Savior was healing and loving people* who were bearing clubs, torches, and swords.

This is an example for us. Through faith, focus, and love, we may serve one another—we may see the horizon's light through a threatening storm and come to fully trust and give thanks for the sovereignty and salvation of our Lord.

There are so many ways and directions our attention can be swayed by the world and circumstances of the day. It is even more likely that our attention will be diverted resulting in worry and anger when we put our trust in anything or anyone, but God. When God is not first in our lives, "our daily bread" can

43

become complaint and discontent. Storm days have a way of dimming the light. The darkness can set the tone and expectation for the day. However, days of storm can also draw us closer together and closer to God when we realize how little in life matters without each other and without Him. We become stronger in discovering our refuge in the storm is Him. He is faithful even in the darkest storm and daily turmoil.

People change as do conditions, cultures and creeds, but God stays the same. Some believe our God needs to be modernized and made-over in order to be more contemporary and relevant to our time. Changing God to fit into our world, instead of changing to fit into His is like choosing the storm instead of the light. It is as if His inspired Word from Genesis, "In the beginning," (Genesis 1:1) to Revelation, "Amen," (Revelation 22:21) needs a fashionable spin. That would be like finding a crop that can feed a starving world, but plowing it under or changing its ingredients to meet the appetite of the day—or Israelites waking one morning to find manna from heaven just outside of their tents and asking, "What else have you got?"

We are placed into our time and days, relationships, and locations by Christ Jesus for a reason. It is not to blend in and get by but to stand out and trust God. That does not mean we have to be a star at something or change the world. However, we should recognize and confess to others that our God is the source of every miraculous sunrise—it is only by His Spirit, power, and provision we live—and that by His love in us, we offer His love through us to all He entrusts to us.

Whether we share this from the rooftop or live it out among our family and friends, it is foundational to what we stand upon and to how we grow to fulfill God's plan for our life. His calling for us is different for everyone, but there is majestic power, purpose, and presence that weaves them together and *connects us to one another: HIM!*

He is the Source and Author of us all. The answer to our life's purpose is always available from Him. Seeking His direction and obeying His command is not easy to do without trust in Him as our Creator, Sustainer, and Redeemer. In the absence of trusting God, finding our purpose may not happen in our lifetime. He has given us individuality and free will. It is not uncommon to take these gifts and think we are the author of our own plan, the provider of our own means and controller of our own destiny. We may think we earn it all by our own ability and the power of our will.

One day when we meet our Lord face to face, our life's purpose and blessings given into our care will clearly come into view, whether we recognized, sought, obeyed, and fulfilled His direction or not. How we long to hear Him say, "Well done good and faithful servant" (Matthew 25:21). The thought of that meeting and its range of outcomes may raise some big issues for us. First is acknowledgement that we work for Him. He is the source of all we have. Second, we are accountable for what we do, and there are consequences. Some of us may ask, "Is this true?" We all make mistakes and get off course sometimes, but Christ Jesus came to save and not condemn. The following encounter with Jesus recorded in the Gospel of John may help clarify this point:

Motivated by a desire to discredit Jesus and bring charges against Him for failure to uphold Mosaic Law, a crowd brought a woman to Him who had been caught in the act of adultery. They said to Jesus, "Moses commanded us to stone such. What do you say about her?" (John 8:5)

The fact they did not bring the man who was with her or produce any witnesses, both of which the Law required, confirmed the crowd cared nothing for this human being. The Lord responded in wisdom and love for her and them by saying, "*Let* him who is without sin among you be the first to cast a stone at her" (John 8:7).

One by one the conspirators and accusers dropped their stones and walked away leaving only the woman and Jesus remaining. Our Lord looked at her and said, "Woman, where are they? Has no one condemned you?" (John 8:10) She said, "No one, Lord." Our Savior replied, "Neither do I condemn you—go, and do not sin again" (John 8:11).

In this brief life or death encounter, the amazing grace of our Lord makes several things clear. First, it is not mistakes we make, it is sin. Second, it is not getting off course, it is choosing the course we take. Third, by condemning someone else, we convict ourselves—and thanks be to God, Christ does save.

The most significant moment of our life is our meeting with Christ Jesus. He does not condemn. We do that all by ourselves by the words of our mouth, the content of our heart, and the choices we make. What a relief it is to know we do not have to make a defense. The woman did not say, "It was only one time" or, "there were extenuating circumstances" or, "nobody got hurt" or, "times have changed." She didn't offer a word. What comfort to know there will be no question with whom we are meeting that day. The woman did not require an introduction to recognize and confess Jesus as Lord. Imagine the peace that overcame her when her accusers' shouts and demands ended, and the inexpressible joy she felt knowing her sin did not define her life, but a day and a meeting with her Lord did. What a great day for her, and that day awaits us.

It is important, however, not to overlook what else our Lord said—"Do not sin again." He not only saved her but gave her direction that, if followed, would keep her safe. With His heart of forgiveness and His knowledge of the dangers she would face, He warned her not to go there again. This was not a passing remark, but the last word He spoke to her. It was not just "go," but *"go and do not sin again."*

Why stress this? It must have been clear to her how close she came to death. Like all of God's inspired Scripture, the words our Lord spoke were not for her benefit alone. They are for us in our day as well. We are so far removed from those ancient times and thoughts about sin. Perhaps, this distance explains issues about the relevancy of God's Word and warnings about sin. After all, codes of conduct and standards to uphold are concepts of antiquity that just don't apply like they once did. Or do they?

Elected officials swear to uphold the Constitution. Doctors take an oath to do no harm. The symbol of the criminal justice system is a blindfolded woman holding a scale. Agriculture and food-handling regulations are fundamental to public health. And the value of gold bullion is a standard that impacts the world. Other codes also apply to everyday life. There is zero tolerance of drugs, guns, and bullies in our schools. Our employers and unions have rules of behavior and performance written into policies and contracts. Public safety officials have rules they are sworn to honor and enforce.

Our first experience with rules and obedience, however, came much earlier in life. Mom and dad said, "Don't talk to strangers. Don't touch the hot stove. Don't run with scissors. Look both ways before crossing the street. Clean your room. Be home by 10 p.m." Thou shall and thou shall not is pretty clear no matter how we look at it.

All of these, and more, are in place and upheld for our good. Some with our consent, others not, but we expect consequences should they be disobeyed. What they all have in common is a source of authority we either reject or obey. Is it possible our compliance is based on our consent and approval of the standard? After all, we create our rules—God creates His. Ours are for our reasons—God's are for His. Ours are for our time—God's are for all time.

Authority is something we have taken issue with for generations, particularly when it comes to God. *History is replete with rejection of Him and His authority.* We prefer deciding for ourselves what is right or wrong or whether there are any absolutes at all. What we accept or reject is a matter of our choosing. However, there is a far greater difference than the source and authority of rule. The difference is sin and what it does. It breaks God's heart and His sacred standards. It separates us from Him, and it separates us from each other.

There are countless explanations for crime, social injustice, abusive relationships, and societal views of life. Imagine no murder, lying, stealing, or covetousness—no child abuse, road rage or rape—no homelessness, hunger, illiteracy, prejudice, or hate. We have never known what life would like if we had upheld God's rules. However, we have a lot of experience with the reality of being separated from each other by breaking them. We may look around and think, "We are not so bad—in fact, we are pretty good."

Do we expect employers to reward employees for willful violations of policies or schools to reward students who skip classes or parents to reward children for blatant disobedience? Probably not, yet we want God to reward and reunite us with each other in spite of our disobedience to Him. Consider what we expect of those who are closest to us. We expect their loyalty and support—we expect their availability and willingness to stand with us even when others do not. *Do we apply these standards to ourselves in our relationship with God?*

We can be so consumed by our day, so familiar and comfortable with our setting, responsibilities, and relationships that we confuse who we are with the job we do. We give little and

sometimes no thought to whom we belong, who we are supposed to be, and what we are supposed to do.

First, we are God's. Not believing this or abandoning it changes
everything. Our blessing as His child can become null and
void if that is our choice. Esau sold his birthright to his brother
Jacob for a bowl of stew. In doing so, he satisfied his temporal
hunger and later wept upon realizing the eternal blessing he
could not recover.

As children of God and brothers and sisters with each other,
we are to love and care for our family—forgiving, giving and
praying for one another always. Just as members of families
do. *We are to live like we know to whom we belong,* perhaps, by
what we do or by the person we are becoming, but for each of
us it is by keeping in mind that we belong to God and making it
a personal priority to honor and obey Him. Psalm 23 is known
and beloved around the world:

> The Lord is my shepherd, I shall not want—He
> makes me lie down in green pastures. He leads
> me beside still waters—He restores my soul. He
> leads me in paths of righteousness for His names
> sake. Even though I walk through the valley of
> the shadow of death, I fear no evil—for Thou
> art with me—Thy rod and Thy staff they com-
> fort me. Thou preparest a table before me in the
> presence of my enemies—Thou anointest my
> head with oil, my cup overflows. Surely good-
> ness and mercy shall follow me all the days of
> my life—and I shall dwell in the house of the
> Lord forever.

This reminds us that *we are guided and cared for by the Good
Shepherd,* Christ Jesus. Even when we wander away from Him,

as we all sometimes do, He seeks us out, comes to our rescue, and guides us safely home.

The direction our Lord gave the woman accused of adultery was to "go—and do not sin again." This applies to us, as well, because we fail in so many ways characterized by unfaithfulness. In the Scripture cited, adultery was infidelity to the sacredness of marriage. In our life, it is infidelity to each other, it is infidelity to our life purpose, and it is infidelity to God. Yet, even the heartbreaking experience of infidelity does not create a storm without hope of recovery.

The prophet Hosea loved his wife (a picture of God's love for us) even when she was repeatedly and knowingly unfaithful to him. Nevertheless, Hosea was not without hope. Hopelessness is coming to a point when evidence, facts, and what we see lead us to conclude nothing will change in our home, school, work, or in the world. It is coming to terms with conditions as they are and no longer believing in life as it could be. It is giving into the temptation not to hope, giving up on seeing God's purpose fulfilled in our lives. Doing so produces lives without hope. Life without hope, is life without knowing the Good Shepherd is ours, and we are His.

The evidence and facts of the crucifixion, death, and burial of Christ Jesus were indisputable to people who witnessed it. It happened just as Isaiah had prophesied seven hundred years before Jesus was born, and as Jesus Himself said it would. Then came the third day when He rose from the dead. Many failed to see that coming. It can be hard to believe something we have not experienced or seen ourselves.

The day of Jesus' Resurrection and in the days that followed, many who were unbelieving came to believe. Hopelessness became joyfulness. The lost became assured. People in hiding boldly spoke out. Faithlessness changed to faithfulness and fear to strength. All this happened because they saw the risen Lord and believed.

Jesus had told them He would rise, but they, and we, tend to rely on our expectation and experience. Seeing anything more requires faith. It requires a selfless perspective embodied in Christ Jesus. People then, and now, can see with His eyes and Spirit beyond the headlines to the extraordinary significance of every woman, man and child, the beauty of every hill and valley, and the miraculous gift of every sunrise.

The prophet Habakkuk inquired of God, asking why the people of God were not being disciplined for their disobedience and unbelief. God answered, "I am doing a work in your days that you would not believe if I told you" (Habakkuk 1:5). So He was then, and so He is now. One way He works in and through us is with sacred stewardships in our care. We often think of discipline as some form of punishment, but it is also teaching, caring, and growing. All of these are part of sacred stewardships. It is love selflessly offered for someone or something else. It may not be seen and received by everyone that way, but that's okay. To be seen by one another is not the motive. The motive is to serve the calling God puts on our hearts whether people value or acknowledge it or not. The point is faithfulness to God. He sees.

What is the outcome of the work we are doing in our days for Him? It may not be what we expect, which is why we would not believe it if He told us. The Lord sees the end from the beginning and *"His thoughts are much higher than ours"* (Isaiah 55:9). We may not know the reason or result of our sacred stewardship until our one-on-one meeting with Christ Jesus. It may be the people, resources, and days we have the opportunity and privilege to serve. It may be preparation and readiness for future plans He is yet to reveal.

The week introduced in Genesis is not just a pattern of time that we repeat in our day—it is also a reference to our future. At the end of each day of creation, "there was evening and there was morning, one day" (Genesis 1:5). Then came a second day, evening and morning. So it was for every day through the sixth, an evening and a morning and "behold it was very good" (Genesis 1:31). Each day had a beginning and an end, just like every day of our lives. When God rested from all He had created, there is no reference to evening or morning. There is no reference to this *one day* as ever ending. There is no reference to time.

For all who believe, *this is the day of our salvation*. It is the day we see how God has always seen us. It is the day we see what is truly selfless, merciful, and honoring to God in us and what is not. It is the day of reunion, praise, prayer, and love. It is the day of reflection, thanksgiving, and worship like never before. It is the day to understand and celebrate all Christ Jesus has done, is doing, and will do. It is the day when once and for all we are free from our sins. It is the day on bended knee *we are given a new name and renewed purpose*. It is the day we feast with the King of kings. It is the day of unspeakable joy that is full of glory. It is the day faith is seen face to face. All of our days lead to this day.

Yet, we generally do not give it much thought or preparation. We are more likely to be preoccupied with life as we know it: what we hear, see, and do. In fact, we spend days, weeks, or even months planning and preparing for a vacation or some other important activity. We make sure everything is ready, and we are set. We leave nothing to chance. After all, we want to make the most of the time and opportunity that lies ahead. Wasting even one day is unimaginable. Thoughts about leaving the world and situation we are familiar with—the people we love and things we do, for a day and place without end is not the same as anticipating a vacation. For one thing, vacations are temporary, and we return home. For some, getting back home is the best part of the trip. Christ Jesus told us why, *"Where your treasure is, there will your heart be also"* (Matthew 6:21).

Home is where the people, places, and priorities we treasure are found. It is something into which we invest much of our life and resources. It is where we can truly be ourselves. It is the base that we set out from each day and where we long to return for rest. It is where we are loved, not because of what we do or who we are, but because no matter what we do or who we are, we are always loved. It is where we live, laugh, grow, and cry. It is where we recover from illness and injury, and find shelter and peace. Like no other place, it occupies a unique space in our heart. We can see it inside and out with great clarity, no matter how far away it may be. When distance or circumstance separates us from it for periods of time, we know loved ones are there making ready, waiting, and anticipating our homecoming.

As wonderful as our temporary home in the world is, *the Spirit of God imparts to our spirit knowledge of our eternal home* with these words: "What no eye has seen, nor ear heard, nor the heart of man conceived, what God has prepared for those who love Him" (1 Corinthians 2:9). Think of all the beauty and joy we have seen, heard, and experienced in the world, yet God's Word says we have never seen, heard or conceived of anything like what awaits us in heaven.

God's Word teaches us to "Lay up for yourselves treasures in Heaven where neither moth nor rust consumes and where thieves do not break in and steal" (Matthew 6:20). The treasures we love so much now will pass away, but those in heaven remain vibrant and alive.

This can be pictured with our trees. We water and protect a tree planted in memory of a loved one or for the birth of a child and are thrilled by its growth and presence in our life. But a day comes when we may no longer be able to care for it, yet it remains firmly rooted, yielding benefits for many families for years to come. They may have no idea of its history, planting, or the one it honors—even so, the provisions and shelter it provides continue to impact lives long after we are gone.

In a similar way, we can gather and count the number of apples produced by one tree, but we cannot begin to number the apples that may come from just one of its precious seeds. Trees are like that. The one who plants and waters does so in faith. The One who creates and gives the growth sees the end from the beginning. All they produce by God's mighty hand only He sees fully, for now. So it is with sacred stewardships. We wait to see how they abound to His glory.

A day is coming, as Jesus tells us, "In that day you will know I am in my Father, and you in me, and I in you" (John 14:20). All of our sacred stewardships, all of our brothers and sisters in Christ from every nation and time, all of the treasures laid up, all of the glory that abounds—all vibrant, joyful, and everlasting, will be in the presence and source of the first light of creation, our eternal light, the foundational light of Genesis: *One Lord, one family, one day!*

Chapter 5

For This I Was Born

A ndrea Bocelli is a magnificent singer. One of the many songs he performs so beautifully is entitled "When a Child Is Born." The spirit and lyrics of the song capture the remarkable and transformational impact of every child's life. The message resonates in our hearts for many reasons, at every stage of life, whether we are parents or not. One reason is the feeling that can sweep over us when we see and hold a newborn. This precious gift of God, from the moment of conception, a human being, flesh of our flesh and bone of our bone, is entrusted to our protection and love. It is then that we may begin to understand how much the world and our life has changed for the better, and forever, by this one uniquely gifted little child. The thought then enters our mind how unimaginable life would be without them.

It may also be the moment we understand how our parents felt when we were born: a combination of anticipation, joy, and profound responsibility. Perhaps it is when we truly begin to realize all they did for us. As we grew up and grew away from them to make a home of our own, they were always cheering and praying for fulfillment of God's plan for our life: the reason we were born.

Christ Jesus said, "For this I was born, and for this I have come into the world, to bear witness to the truth" (John 18:37). He came to the world and to the people He had created, though He existed from eternity past, as the firstborn son of a teenage girl

55

and a humble carpenter, both of whom loved God and honored His Word. Imagine this young couple discovering their purpose was to raise the Son of God.

Consider the Lord Himself, submitting to their direction and honoring them and their rules though He was Creator, Sustainer, and Savior of their lives. Clarity of purpose allows us to accomplish many things, even what may seem unlikely, if not impossible. Mary and Joseph embody this. They were without the care or support of family and friends or even in possession of a modest room the night our Lord was born. After His birth they fled to Egypt in accordance with God's Word to protect the child from Herod, who ordered "the death of every male child in Bethlehem two years old and younger," (Matthew 2:16) in an effort to destroy the Lord. A young woman with her son and husband crossed a desert that night not knowing what the future would hold, but knowing they were fleeing for their child's life and were trusting in God's care. After the threat had passed, an Angel of the Lord said it was safe to go home, so they returned to Galilee and made a life for their family in Nazareth. Imagine a woman of that day who was thought to have conceived out of wedlock, while she was betrothed, and not by the man she would marry. Their neighbors' suspicion, condemnation, and shame may have accompanied Mary and Joseph all of their days, yet through it all, *they fulfilled their purpose* and raised *God with us*.

They were never out of the will of God or beyond His mercy and grace. What encouragement this is for all of us as we live to fulfill His purpose for our life. It is important to note that their life was not easy or perhaps even comfortable. Joseph undoubtedly worked hard to support his growing family, and Mary was not likely a member of the accepted social order of the day.

Because we are in God's will is not a guarantee that everything will be good. Christ Jesus said, "If any man would come after me, let him deny himself and take up his cross and follow me"

(Matthew 16:24). This does not sound like an invitation to a life of ease and accolades. It sounds more like hardship and sacrifice.

Jesus told His disciples "Remember the word that I said to you. A servant is not greater than his master. If they persecuted me, they will persecute you—if they kept my word, they will keep yours also" (John 15:20). As followers of Christ Jesus, the apostles counted it glory to suffer for His sake. When they were mocked and ill-treated, they rejoiced in the knowledge they were in God's will. Some people with whom they shared the Gospel did receive and keep their word, but their word and message was not their own. The message was the Lord's who commissioned the apostles, and everyone who believes, to share it with the whole world.

The voice we listen to makes all the difference to the words and message we live and share. Is it the Lord's or the world's? They are not difficult to tell apart. One exalts Christ Jesus—one does not. One is based on God's sovereignty and creative design, the other on happenstance and random chance. One believes the Bible—one says it is myth. One honors God's commandments—one wants them removed from public space. One forgives—one holds a grudge. One is humility—the other pride. One says the best is yet to be—the other says get all you can right now. One is about God's plan—the other is about ours. One trusts God—the other trusts ourselves. One gives without expecting payment—the other receives without giving. One says God created us to serve Him—the other says God doesn't need us. One is a commitment to love—one is love without commitment. One is for all time—the other changes with the times. One is peace, the other anxiety. One proclaims freedom from sin—one says there is no sin. One is resurrection to life in Christ—one is separation from Him. One is by faith—one is by force.

Our reason for living and serving has much to do with who and what we give our heart to. It is possible we may view the person, or purpose, as being temporary and conditional, based on how things work out. If that is the case, then we never really gave our heart in the first place, and who or what we live for today may have nothing to do with who or what we live for tomorrow. With such a view and choice comes personal acknowledgment that the people, places, and priorities of our life are disposable. In effect, we are hedging our bets, keeping our options open so that in the event something better comes along, we can move on with no second thoughts or regret. This is the opposite of being "all in." It says what is most important to me is me. Why would we be entrusted life by Christ Jesus to make ourselves the focus of life?

A focus on self has either forgotten, never knew, or perhaps disbelieves something foundational to life in the Spirit. Christ Jesus came to us as a humble servant, leaving the glory of Heaven as God the Son, to obey the will of God the Father in the power of God the Holy Spirit to serve and save us. *Living to serve others applies to us* as well. Our lives are lived in service of one kind or another. What we choose to focus on, self-love or selfless love, is up to us. Self-love is and always has been a powerful motivator, understandably so. As children it came naturally. When we were told to share our toys, we may have stashed some away like a squirrel leaving caches of acorns here and there for the winter. The fact we had not played with some for a while made it no easier to surrender them. Even when sharing, we may have wanted them back as soon as mom and dad stepped out of the room.

Adults can be even less enthusiastic about giving what they value away, particularly with a joyful heart. How often in church has the pastor said the Lord loves a cheerful giver as the offering plate is about to be passed? There may be times we feel it is more of a duty or compulsion than a joy and a blessing to return to the Lord some of the abundance He has given to us. Or how often do we feel it is not enough, or maybe it's too much, when it is the spirit of the giver that matters to God.

Self-love is gaining prominence. With so much encouragement of it in the world and validation of it by people we admire and aspire to be like, it is a well-established and celebrated point of view. Followers of Christ Jesus, however, aspire to be more like Him. His life epitomizes selfless love. It is pictured by the father's embrace of the prodigal son, the one who sought his inheritance before his father's passing. The father yielded to his son's request though it grieved him. It is seen again in the account of Job refusing to curse God. Even his wife said, "Curse God and die" (Job 2:9). Despite unimaginable suffering, Job did not place his afflictions ahead of reverence for God. Likewise, when Christ Jesus called Zacchaeus by name, this overwhelmed and overjoyed Jewish tax collector who worked for Rome quickly climbed down from his perch in a tree where he sought to get a glimpse of Jesus passing by. The Lord made Himself available, again, to someone in need. Zacchaeus unconditionally opened his heart and home to the Lord. *Selfless love climbs out on a limb.*

The Lord left eternal glory to step into time and space to live and die for us, as one of us. He was tempted in every way, as we are, yet without sin—a man of sorrows and grief, yet without self-love. He is the Savior of the world yet was rejected and condemned by it, and He is the Creator and Sustainer of life yet was unwilling to save Himself from being judged, mocked, beaten, shamed, and crucified. For He loved them and all of us even before our birth, and all the powerful forces aligned and bearing down on Him on Calvary could not stop Christ Jesus from winning victory over death and clothing us in His righteousness. That is selfless love.

There is no question selfless love may produce personal suffering. Recall what Simon Peter shared with a young and persecuted church. He said, "But even if you do suffer for righteousness sake, you will be blessed. Have no fear of them, nor be troubled, but in your hearts reverence Christ as Lord" (1 Peter 3:14-15). By the power of the Holy Spirit they did. That is selfless love. But how can our Father, who loves each of us so much that He gave His only Son so we could live, allow suffering for His name even in our day?

We may not fully know or understand until we breathe heaven's pure air, but in God's Holy presence, the reason for our suffering, our relationships, the content and motive of our hearts, our sacred stewardships, and the purpose for our lives will be clear. While we are here and suffering for Christ's sake, Peter tells us we will be blessed. Every physical limitation and pain, every loss and sacrifice, and every wrong and wound inflicted to our mind, body, and soul will be set right by Him. That is selfless love, too.

With knowledge that it is not up to us but to Christ Jesus, we can know far more, right here and right now, before we are in His presence, about why we were born. It is to learn to rely on Him in good times and bad. It is to trust His will whether we understand it or not. It is to remember and give Him thanks for all He has done and our opportunities to serve Him. It is to cast every fear upon Him. It is to submit to His sovereignty and give Him praise. It is to confess our sins and to repent. It is to know He appoints times for rain, for sun, and for plants to grow, and they obey. It is to seek His guidance and help in prayer. It is to listen for and expect His reply. It is to conform to His likeness and follow Him. It is to live with Him and embody His selfless love.

Think of the unimaginable and unseen expanse of the universe and of the timelessness of eternity and the infinite glory and power of God. *Our Creator, Christ Jesus, made each of us unique and our purpose distinct because He creates endlessness.* We reflect, in part, the extraordinary miracle and intricacy of life He has wrought in every person, every color, every spirit, every calling, and every display of His love. We are individuals, but we are also members with each other of a great family when we accept Him as Lord. Like members of a family, no two are endowed with the same gifts or with the same purpose for their life.

Infinite glory and power may be a concept we struggle to understand, but it is the very heart and Spirit of our God, who has always been and always is and always will be. It is not difficult or unreasonable for Him to prepare us for a particular purpose, or to inspire and guide us, to equip and empower us, and to counsel and deliver us in every moment of our lives. Our part is to want to serve Him. With that we need nothing more because with that He provides all we need.

That does not mean it will be easy. In fact, there is reason and evidence to believe it will be difficult. Just recall how Joseph's brothers sold him into captivity and lied to their father about his disappearance. Consider Nehemiah with a trowel in one hand to build a wall, and sword in the other to defend the city. Gideon's troops went from thousands to a few hundred and were delivered by God's hand. Ruth was scavenging the fields owned by another to gather what she and her mother-in-law needed to survive. The great prophet Elijah, who called fire down from heaven, immediately afterward ran for his life for fear of Jezebel. Jonah ran from God rather than participate in the greatest revival the world has ever seen. God's inspired call on their lives did not promise ease.

Christ Jesus made in a single drop of water such vast capacity and value that if every molecule it contained were converted to a grain of sand, there would be enough material to create a road from New York to San Francisco, a half mile wide and one foot thick. (*Minneapolis Star*, "Our Amazing Universe," Lee

Rodgers quoted by Bob Murphy) Jesus did this with a drop of water. Imagine the capacity He placed in each of us.

So whether we have brothers like Joseph's or if we are working to restore something like Nehemiah or we are leading people into battle like Gideon or maybe like Ruth, we are living day to day by faith or like Elijah, we have high visibility and command or like Jonah, we have a message to share, in God's providential purpose, there is no telling what we may be blessed to do for Him, for each other, and for all He entrusts to our care. Joseph had the privilege of helping to save the known world—Nehemiah, the honor of working to restore the City of God—Gideon, the distinction of winning a war against all odds—Ruth, the blessing of being in the direct line of God's royal family—Elijah, the ascension into heaven though he never died—and Jonah, the miracle of witnessing the world's most powerful nation turn their hearts and worship to God.

What may our purpose for God be? If we don't know, we should ask Him. We should be in His Word. We should identify, cultivate, and share, through trusted coaching and mentorships, gifts He has given to our care. We should anticipate His help in all we do for His glory. *With a grateful heart, we can take daily steps with Him and trust His leading in our lives.*

Continually seek His will and know that He has something specific for us to do, as He did for faithful women and men recorded for us in Scripture. Be vigilant to resist the thought we can never be anything more than we are. The only way that may be true is if we choose to live apart from God, have no desire or confidence to serve Him, or we elect to ignore or reject His call. Even then, He may not accept our refusal, as was the case with Jonah.

Even in those times we may feel alone, overlooked, or unvalued, that is not true as long as we trust God. The Lord knows about all the blessings of service and relationships He will yet provide which is testimony to the truth: the best is yet to be. What man may mean for evil, God uses for good. That has always been true and still is. Our challenge, in the flesh, is to never forget God is present and faithful through all time. We are mistaken if we hope He will conform to our view instead of conforming to His. We are vulnerable and weak when we regard Him as an option, rather than as our fortress and Savior.

Remember what Christ Jesus said to Peter, James, and John in the garden of Gethsemane, *"The spirit indeed is willing but the flesh is weak"* (Matthew 26:41). He knows we are weak and fall short, but He is always near to help us back to our feet. We just need to give Him our trust and follow His leading.

The prophet Jeremiah was imprisoned by his own people for his testimony and warning to them from God, which they did not want to hear and could not believe because false prophets had proclaimed peace. Jeremiah feared for his life, yet he wept for his people because he loved them and knew what was ahead. King Zedekiah sought the words of God spoken to Jeremiah and secretly pledged before the living God—no harm would come to the prophet if he hid nothing from the king. Jeremiah told the king if he obeyed God, Jerusalem would not be destroyed by Babylon and that the king and his household would live. If he failed to heed and follow God's Word, the city would be destroyed, and he and his family would not escape.

Zedekiah feared the Jews who had deserted to the Chaldeans and what they might do to him, so instead of obeying God's Word, he chose to flee with his family in the hope he would live. He and his family were captured. He had failed to see and believe. The result was fatal for his family and disastrous for his city. He was blinded literally and spiritually. However the king of Babylon treated Jeremiah with respect and commanded that no harm come to him. Unknown to the king of Babylon, he fulfilled, by God's grace, the pledge King Zedekiah had made to Jeremiah, that he would be safe.

The similarity between Zedekiah and Jeremiah is both feared for their lives. The difference is Jeremiah trusted and followed the Lord's leading—King Zedekiah did not.

We have the same decision to make. We can seek, receive, and follow God's direction for our life and the sacred stewardships in our care, or we can seek, listen to, and follow someone else's. *Only the Spirit of God, though, can convict our spirit* and provide assurance that we may truly know, *for this I was born.*

Chapter 6

No Way!

How often have we considered something, or maybe been told or heard something that was so incredible or unexpected our first thought was simply "No way!"

Think for moment about the prophet Jeremiah. God spoke to him when Jeremiah was a young boy and said, "Before I formed you in the womb I knew you, and before you were born I consecrated you—I appointed you a prophet to the nations" (Jeremiah 1:5). Can you imagine what Jeremiah must have thought? The Creator of the universe speaking to him and saying in effect, "Young man, I have a job for you to do."

Or, how about what God said to Noah: "Make yourself an ark of gopher wood;" (Genesis 6:14) a storm is on the way. Talk about a big job and a culture that wanted nothing to do with it. Or Abram, who was from a well-established and successful family living in the thriving culture of Haran, hearing God say, "Go from your country and your kindred and your father's house to the land I will show you" (Genesis 12:1). He had never been to Canaan—he had no idea what he was getting into. He just packed his things and headed out. Who does that?

To Moses, an eighty-year-old shepherd who had fled from Pharaoh forty years earlier, God said, "I will send you to Pharaoh that you may bring forth my people, the sons of Israel out of

Egypt" (Exodus 3:10). A run-away shepherd was headed for a showdown with the most powerful man on the planet. No wonder Moses suggested Aaron, his brother, was better suited for the job.

Saul, on the road to Damascus, where he met the risen Christ for the first time learned Jesus was calling him to become His appointed apostle to the Gentiles. Saul, the man who hated followers of Christ Jesus would become their beloved apostle Paul. No way!

We can bring this much closer to home by looking in the mirror at the expression on our face, and the challenge in our heart with God's call and direction to us. We can experience, first-hand, the feeling of, "You want me to do what?" Christ Jesus calls us to love our enemies and pray for those who treat us wrong. You have got to be kidding! Sometimes it's hard enough just to be civil to people we disagree with, don't like, and who stand for something we disdain. Yet, we are supposed to love them and pray for them? It might be easier to build that ark.

Before we look for gopher wood and begin construction, let's consider what we are building. Our way, we build bunkers. Jesus' way, we build bridges. Our way, we build animosity. Jesus' way, we build civility. *Our way, we build bitterness. Jesus' way, we build forgiveness.* Our way, we build retribution. Jesus' way, we build mercy. Our way, we build greed. Jesus' way, we build grace. Our way, we build disbelief. Jesus' way, we build trust. Our way, we build disrespect. Jesus' way, we build honor. Our way, we build division. Jesus' way, we build relationships. Our way, we build life as it's always been: me against you, we against them—and our children learn from us how to respond with anger and "in your face" to someone or something they don't agree with or like. Jesus' way, we build a new life.

Isaiah prophesied that the wolf, leopard, lion, and lamb would live together in peace, and there would be no hurt or destruction among them. He answered the question, "How can this be?" when he said, "For the earth shall be full of the knowledge of the Lord as the waters cover the sea" (Isaiah 11:9). A time is coming when there will be no more predator and prey, no more fear or hiding, no more victims, no more suffering or dying, and no more hate or violence.

No way! The history of the world since the days of Cain and Abel could be characterized with a clenched fist. If we don't get our way, then we demand it or take it one way or another. We see it in our politics, news, and entertainment. We see it on our roads, communities, and business practices. We hear it in our speeches, shouts, and sermons. We live it in our hospitals, shelters, and courts. We may even see it in the mirror as we try to cover up wounds received or perhaps inflicted. It is right there, in our face.

But there are also many people all around the world who follow another pattern. Young men and women volunteer to serve as big brothers and big sisters. Adults open their homes and hearts and share genuine hospitality with visitors and stranded travelers. Doctors, nurses, and technicians leave their hospitals and families to care for people in countries and conditions far different than their own. Families share love, safety, and resources with foster children. Seniors knit and make gifts for people they may never meet. People donate their time and "know how" to travel to scenes of human suffering in order to rebuild structures and restore lives. Countless people serve in their neighborhoods to help each other. Millions donate funds and talent to causes, organizations, and people who save lives. Millions more of all ages, backgrounds, and means give hope, encouragement, resources, guidance, training, love, and prayers without expecting or asking for anything in return.

The pattern we choose becomes the foundation of the life we build and live. King Solomon followed his father King David to the throne of Israel. The son's mandate was to build the temple of God and to keep God's ordinances. Scripture identifies David as, "a man after God's own heart" (1 Samuel 13:14). He counseled his son to keep God's Word. The pattern was passed from father to son—Solomon agreed. God gave Solomon wisdom and knowledge to rule the people. King Solomon is said to be the wisest man who ever lived. He summarized what he learned throughout his life with these words at the end of the Book of Ecclesiastes: "Fear God, and keep His commandments—for this is the whole duty of man" (Ecclesiastes 12:13).

Earlier in his reign the new king provided directions to build the temple of God. He shared design specifications including intricate details of every feature of the temple with a man named Huram-abi, an extraordinary craftsman. He along with many highly skilled and devoted people built a magnificent temple. Where did the plan and purpose come from? Everything from the height, width, and breadth of the temple to its windows, doors, floors, curtains, and utensils—every detail—was specified by God, and Solomon followed it to the letter. When it was finished, he called all the families of Israel to assemble to dedicate the temple and instructed them to keep God's Word.

The problem was, with all of his wisdom, knowledge, and love of God, King Solomon did not keep God's Word. He did the very things God told him not to do, similar to the decision Adam and Eve made. God said to Adam, "You may freely eat of every tree of the garden—but of the tree of the knowledge of good and evil you shall not eat, for in the day that you eat of it you shall die" (Genesis 2:16-17). Both King Solomon and Adam knew what God said. They understood His direction. They knew the consequence of not keeping His Word, as well as the blessing of keeping it, yet neither could curb their own appetite or desires.

These men had remarkable relationships with God. They talked with Him, revered Him, blessed Him, and were blessed by Him—yet, at crossroad moments of their lives, they made choices they knew were outside of God's will. Solomon was in charge of building an amazing temple to exacting specifications. Adam was in charge of the most extraordinary garden on earth. Yet neither could take charge of himself.

Before coming to any conclusions about the moral character of these two men, *consider all the crossroads we have come to* in our life and which way we went. The truth is, it is easier to follow complicated blueprints for construction of a building or to care for a pristine garden than to keep the Word of God without fail.

The apostle Paul, in his letter to the Romans, said, "None is righteous, no, not one" (Romans 3:10). If these words were in any book other than the Bible, that may seem pretty difficult to believe. Of the billions of people alive, or who have lived in the past, it would seem someone, somewhere, sometime, must have been righteous. Consider the Bible's meaning of righteousness: being right with God. Christ Jesus was righteous without sin, but Paul is not talking about our Lord—he's talking about himself and all of us.

Believing God's Word is the challenge. How can we live God's Word in our lives, in our relationships and in all we do if we do not believe it is true? Loving our enemies is a tall order. Investing our time and spirit in prayer for them is, also. Even if we accept the thought that it is the proper thing to do, doing it faithfully in truth and with love requires far more than acceptance. It requires deep foundational belief that what God says, He means, and what He says is true.

Since the time of Adam and Eve, there has always been someone who says, "That is not what God means," or "Surely that will not happen," or "That is not my interpretation," or "That is not the God I believe in," or "The Bible has been corrupted by man;" or "You don't really believe that stuff, do you?" If we are not living God's Word as best we can, or at least trying to, and if we are not convicted in our spirit when we fail to, or at least have noticed—and if we have no desire to repent or at least give it thought, how can we say we believe God's Word?

Do we, like King Solomon and Adam, love and believe the Lord and want to honor Him in our life, but also want to do what we choose? Do we feel some kind of regret or seek some intervention or advice when we knowingly disobey His Word, and upon receiving it and feeling better, go back to doing the same thing again? Or, do we not worry about it? Do we doubt God's Word or follow after other words and ways more compatible with our view and with our world?

If the answer to these questions is, "yes," then the answer to the question, "You don't really believe that stuff, do you?" may be one of the following: "I believe some of it. I do not believe any of it. I am not sure what I believe. I believe its meaning and relevance changes with time and circumstance. I believe it is part of the truth, but not all of the truth. I believe my interpretation is what matters. I believe something else is true."

How does our answer compare with what Christ Jesus said? "For this I was born, and for this I have come into the world, to bear witness to the truth" (John 18:37). This remark does not suggest there is another truth or that there is more truth or that truth He gave changes.

How does our answer compare with what the apostle John wrote about Christ Jesus? John said the reason he wrote the Gospel was, "that you may believe" (John 20:31). Nothing in John's words suggest reasons to doubt or deny. His focus is on belief.

70

How does our answer compare with our own view of truth? Is what we believe foundational to our life? Does it have an impact on the way we live? If we flip from one view to another, was the first one true or is the new one right? If the new one is right, what was the first one? And what happens to the new one when another takes its place? Is truth in constant motion? *Shifting sand and tumbling waves are not foundational.* They are beautiful and appealing in many ways, but they move from place to place and then back again. A true foundation is stable. The sand and waves may cover it for a time, but when the sand has blown away and the waves retreat, the foundation remains. It was there all along, even when we could not see, understand or believe it was true.

Christ Jesus loved his disciple Thomas. Thomas was not with the others when Jesus first appeared to them after His resurrection. The disciples told Thomas, "We have seen the Lord." Thomas replied, "Unless I see in His hands the print of the nails, and place my fingers in the mark of the nails, and place my hand in His side, I will not believe." Eight days later the disciples, including Thomas, were together and Jesus appeared again. Our Lord said to Thomas, "Put your finger here, and see my hands and put out your hand, and place it in my side—do not be faithless, but believing." Thomas answered, "My Lord and my God!" Jesus said, "Have you believed because you have seen me? Blessed are those who have not seen me and yet believe" (John 20:25-29).

Jesus was not criticizing Thomas. He loved His disciple and was answering the yearning of Thomas' heart to believe and to know the truth. Christ Jesus answers the yearning of our heart to know Him and to know the truth. But, believing because of proof is different than believing by faith. Jesus said one is blessed.

Many of us are Thomas-like and need proof, and there is nothing wrong with that. In fact, it was Jesus Himself who selected Thomas to be one of the twelve. None of us should ever put our brain in neutral and stop thinking. Christ Jesus gave us the gift of seeking, discovering, deciding, learning, and moving forward. What He said to Thomas, and to us, in part is: believing requires faith in what we cannot see or touch at the moment, which is something we have all experienced.

There are times in life that the future and what we strive to achieve and hold close seem a long way off. Our first day of school may begin a journey that takes years to complete. Then graduation arrives, and we transition to careers and family. Now our time is gladly devoted to spouse and children while serving our employers and customers. Children become grown and have families of their own and careers come to a close. Completing school, raising a family, and savoring a great career may have seemed, at some point, way beyond our reach. But we trusted (believed), that with God's blessings we would enjoy them all.

Think of Abram, who at the age of seventy-five, left everything he had and set out on a one-way journey to the unknown. God promised him a son, in fact—God changed his name from Abram, the "exalted father," to Abraham, the "father of multitudes," so sure was God's fulfillment of His promise. Yet, it was not until Abraham was ninety-nine years old that God told him that he and his wife, Sarah, would have their son the following year. Abraham laughed, and Sarah did, too. In effect, they were saying, "No way!"

In accordance with God's timing and purpose, Abraham and Sarah's son, Isaac, was born. Even Isaac's name, which means laughter, may have been a daily reminder to his parents that God is faithful and keeps His word. Abraham's descendants became as numerous as the stars of heaven, and Sarah became the mother of nations.

Think of David, a boy who tended his father's sheep, standing up for the glory of God to the fierce warrior, Goliath. Neither the king of Israel nor the army of Israel nor any of its champions put their trust in God for deliverance from this mighty man. Their hearts were afraid and fully on the side of the ledger that said, "No way!" But here comes a boy, just a visitor to the troops, who with a stone and a sling and resolute love for God and faith in God's power, faced a mighty champion and inspired a nation.

Elisha, the prophet, was surrounded by an adversarial army and prayed that his servant's eyes might be opened to see the host of heaven, who were standing by to defend him. However, rather than call this heavenly host to intervene, he prayed that the great multitude that had come to destroy him, be temporarily blinded. And, so they were! Elisha then led them to the heart of Samaria. Upon restoring their sight, the army found they were surrounded by Samaritan troops who asked Elisha if they should slay them. "Set bread and water before them, that they may eat and drink and go to their master" (2 Kings 6:22). What? Let their mortal enemy go? No way! But, they did what Elisha said and were freed.

"No way" is a reaction we may have experienced and succumbed to in our lives. It is understandable when we see with our eyes or let our past experiences predict the future or when we see through the eyes of someone we admire or perhaps through the world's perspective instead seeing as God does. Even when we do try to see with the assurance of God's sovereign power and triumph, there is something or someone that remains whispering or shouting in our ear, "There is *no way!*"

Left to our own resources and our own will, or relying on someone else, that may be true, but when the object of our trust, the source of our strength, and the purpose of our life is to fulfill God's will and call, we can be sure *there is a way.* Christ

Jesus came into the world to bear witness to the truth and to show us how to live. He loves and forgives. He serves and sacrifices. He weeps and saves. He creates and sustains. He prays and feeds. He blesses and intercedes. He speaks and heals. He obeys and honors. He calls and leads. And he does all this and more for the joy set before Him—our salvation.

We can do our best to live as He does, but we need His help every day. Whatever He calls us to do, no matter how impossible it may seem, or how much it may require change, or how unsuited we may feel we are—no matter how young or old, strong or weak, or near or far we are from one another, whether the call is familiar or not, and whatever anyone may say: Christ Jesus promised never to leave us. Praise God! The Creator of the universe is with us. It does not get any better than that!

It took Noah more than one hundred years to build the ark— then it rained. Abraham was almost one hundred years old when Isaac was born. King David was patient for years through King Saul's reign. For a lifetime, Jeremiah prophesied God's Word. Moses went through countless trials in preparation to fulfill God's will. All of them believed, obeyed, and prayed.

God's great gifts of sacred stewardships cannot fail to bring Him glory if we love, trust, and obey Him and resist the temptation to say no way. *With Christ Jesus in us, He can do through us all that is within His will for us.*

Chapter 7

Family Resemblance

*W*hat we hold most dear and live for is often modeled for *us,* first and foremost, by our family, from our appearance to our aptitude, our disposition to our mannerisms, sense of humor to personality, ethics and values, foundation and direction, faith and purpose, fairness and justice, trust and protection, sacrifice and love, preparation and service, reason and meaning, laughter and joy, heritage and legacy, and so much more. Our parents, siblings, grandparents, aunts and uncles, cousins, nieces and nephews, guardians, spouse, children and in-laws, each one, our family by blood, marriage, adoption, and by God's great blessing all influence our lives, and we influence theirs by what we say, do and become. We resemble them and they us, like a parent and child.

Relationships with family and others are foundational to life. Whether married, single, divorced, or estranged from family, or whether we make them a priority or not, even if we have never had a family of our own, we all have vital connections. By them we identify who we are, where we come from, where we are heading, what our goals are, what motivates us, what we believe, and who we serve. Our strengths may be different from theirs, and our weaknesses are, too—but something of them is always in us. Perhaps we recognize it, perhaps not, but they are resident in us by God's design and our memories. Others may see it better than we do.

All of the characteristics and experiences we glean from the many connections we have may not always be good. But, for better or worse, they are part of our history, and they equip us in specific ways to better serve Christ Jesus and one another and to value His plan for our life.

Perhaps, we will serve in the same location we have always been, or in another place Christ Jesus calls us to go. It may be the same place, but a new call, or the same call in a new place, or a new place and a new call. The people, location, and calling we serve will be a blessing, and the experience, people, and place we come from will positively impact everything we do. Our family resemblance will show up in some way through how we serve and care.

The apostle Paul shared everything Christ Jesus entrusted to him with Timothy, a young follower of Christ. Paul referred to Timothy as his "child in the faith" (1 Timothy 1:2), his "brother" (Colossians 1:1), a "servant of Christ" (Philippians 1:1), his "beloved child" (2 Timothy 1:2), and co-author of letters to the Philippians, Colossians, Philemon, and First and Second Thessalonians. Timothy's biological father was Greek and his mother and grandmother, who loved and followed Christ Jesus, were Jewish. Paul described Timothy's mother, Eunice, and grandmother, Lois, as "having a sincere faith" (2 Timothy 1:5) as Timothy did also.

Even so, reminders about the work God is doing in and through us are helpful to hear again. Paul told Timothy:

> Do not be ashamed then of testifying to our Lord, nor of me His prisoner, but take your share of suffering for the Gospel in the power of God, who saved us and called us with a holy calling, not by virtue of our works, but in virtue of His own purpose and the grace which He

gave us in Christ Jesus ages ago—and now has manifested through the appearing of our Savior Christ Jesus, who abolished death and brought life and immortality to light through the Gospel (2 Timothy 1:8-10).

Paul was telling Timothy that the work he, Timothy, was doing was put on his heart by grace through Christ Jesus, and it was a holy calling on his life. Paul invested his heart in mentoring and entrusting Timothy with the Gospel. Would his young protégé follow in Paul's footsteps? Timothy's roots were Greek, Jewish, and Christian. Roman polytheism was the culture of the day. His youthfulness, inexperience, and lack of confidence were getting the best of him. The problems at the church of Corinth, to which he had been sent, were serious and deep, so Timothy retreated to Paul at Ephesus.

What was the family resemblance Timothy manifested in Corinth? Was it Greek, Jewish, Christian, or something else? The Bible doesn't say, but we are told that Paul reminded Timothy to "rekindle the gift of God within him." (2 Timothy 1:6) Paul said, "God did not give us a spirit of timidity but a spirit of power and love and self-control" (2 Timothy 1:7).

Was this because Timothy's leadership at Corinth lacked these characteristics so evident in his mentor? What we do know is the apostle Paul confirmed something that Timothy exemplified the rest of his life: (1) his calling was from God—(2) he was "gifted" by God for the calling—and (3) he had a spirit of power, love, and self-control to fully engage in his calling. It is assurance all of us Timothy-like believers need. *We come from God, are gifted by God, and are placed by God's providence in life to serve Him and each other.* And it is not by our virtue or works, but by God's virtue, purpose, and grace He gave us in Christ Jesus ages ago. Upon believing and living this, Timothy became a great champion of Christ and served our Lord as the bishop of the church at Ephesus, a church Paul started on his first missionary trip.

Timothy's family resemblance had characteristics of everyone in his life. They were all part of who he was, where he came from, and how he had been brought up. Each person and place was important to his training, preparation, and fulfillment of God's calling on his life. Timothy's family resemblance was a multi-faceted crystal through which the likeness of God shined bright.

Before Paul and Timothy came to faith in Christ Jesus, there was another young man named Stephen who bore a striking family resemblance to the angelic beings of God. This likeness was identified by the people who were stoning Stephen to death for his testimony and faith in Christ Jesus. Scripture identifies the man who consented to the crowds' stoning, and who stood by witnessing the death of Stephen.

He was Saul of Tarsus, who later became Paul: a preacher, teacher, apostle of Christ, and Timothy's mentor and "father" in the faith. Stephen's brutal stoning and death may have been on Paul's mind when he counseled Timothy to be bold for Christ. It may have been on his mind throughout his life when he thought about Stephen and his participation in Stephen's death. It certainly was a critical part of Paul's experience which he may have reflected on many times. It was also something Paul experienced himself in Lystra, Timothy's hometown.

Like Stephen, Paul was stoned for his testimony of Christ Jesus, and he was left for dead. "But, when the disciples gathered around him he rose and entered the city" (Acts 14:20). Paul could have turned and gone another way, taking up some other line of work, but instead he returned to the city to continue his ministry in the place where those who had just struck him down lived. Paul embodied what he encouraged Timothy to do: "live in the spirit of love, power, and self-control." Whether Timothy witnessed the stoning of Paul or Paul's return to the city, the Bible doesn't say, but what happened to Paul bore a striking family resemblance to his brother in Christ, Stephen.

Even people who bear an unmistakable resemblance to members of their family and who love them with all their heart can withdraw from their family at times to avoid being identified with them. Such was the case with the great apostle Simon Peter. At Antioch, Paul and Peter were sharing the Gospel with Gentiles and were living like them. The apostles taught them, ate meals with them, were a blessing to them, and were blessed by them. They interacted freely and joyfully. But when friends of Peter's arrived who were more legalistic in their views and unfamiliar with sharing their faith or spiritual gifts with people outside their comfort zone, Peter drew back from the Gentiles. Paul called him out on it, in effect saying Peter was a hypocrite and showing partiality. *Peer pressure existed even then.*

Prior to the arrival of this distinguished group of men, Peter was comfortable engaging the Gentiles, but after their arrival he was not. Paul was making public declaration when he corrected Peter by teaching salvation is for everyone who believes and calls upon Jesus' name, Jews and Gentiles alike. Simon Peter knew salvation was free to everyone through Christ Jesus. In fact, he lived it. His devotion to Jesus was genuine and inspiring. Peter exemplified the Lord's commission to share the Gospel with the whole world. The following reflects Peter's heart of reverence and love for our Lord and for every soul to whom he reached out.

When he first met Jesus, Peter said, "Depart from me, for I am a sinful man, O Lord" (Luke 5:8). It was Peter who Jesus commended for his answer to the question, "But who do you, say that I am?" (Mark 8:29) In a boat, on a storm-tossed sea, it was Peter who said, "Lord, if it is you, bid me to come to you on the water" (Matthew 14:28). It was Peter in the Garden of Gethsemane who was willing to fight the multitude to defend our Lord. It was Peter in the courtyard of the high priest while Jesus was being condemned and mocked, who was trying to see what would happen to his Lord. It was Peter who wept over his denial of our Lord. After the Lord's resurrection, it was Peter who had a one-on-one with Jesus and was fully restored.

On the Day of Pentecost, it was Peter who preached boldly to the crowd. He is the apostle an angel of the Lord guided to safety from prison where he was sleeping on the floor, shackled and awaiting his execution the next day. It was Peter who the Lord called to share the Gospel with Cornelius, a Gentile. Cornelius wanted to worship Peter, but Peter said, "Stand up—I too am a man" (Acts 10:26). Peter baptized Cornelius and his whole household in the name of Jesus. Peter was the one whose shadow fell on the sick and they were made well. And it was Peter, greatly inspired by the Holy Spirit, who penned two tremendous letters to the early church. It was this former fisherman, Andrew's older brother, who died like his Savior on a cross but upside down because Peter said he was not worthy to die as Christ Jesus did.

The Lord knew exactly what He was doing when He said to Simon Peter, *"Follow me"* (Matthew 4:19). Even with his incredible heart for the Lord, the family of Christ, and all Jews and Gentiles to whom he preached salvation by faith in Christ Jesus, it was Simon Peter, this great apostle, who apostles and disciples looked to for leadership, who Paul called-out for hypocrisy and partiality for drawing back one time from people with whom he bore such a great family resemblance.

If this criticism can be leveled at Peter, what chances have we to avoid hypocrisy and partiality? Consider some things we allow to separate us from one another: difference of opinions, harsh words, behaviors and attitudes, clothing and appearance, education and status, regions and habits, gender and race, age and beliefs, and memories and history, to name a few. Some of these even create self-imposed absence or a decision by others to distance themselves from someone within their family. What might Paul say?

We can guess what Paul would say, but there is no guesswork involved if we ask ourselves about our own characteristics and who they resemble. Let's say someone, who knew your dad for many years and meets you for the first time, comments, "I knew you were Jim's daughter. You have the same great spirit as your dad." Okay, that narrows it down pretty well. You resemble your father by having his spirit. How about another first meeting that day with another long-time friend of your dad, but this person comments, "Your dad's Italian heritage is alive and well in you." And another person observes, "I can see you love your family, just like your dad."

How is it they all saw something in you that immediately reminded them of your father, but they were different things? Perhaps, it is what they remember best or admire most about your dad. More likely, it is what you said or did and what you have become that reflects your dad. This may come through loud and clear as a result of your nearness to, and love for your father. Do you see what others see of your father in you? Is it obvious to you that you have your dad's spirit, heritage, and priority? Whether you see it or not, if it is there, it identifies you with him.

The opposite can also be true. For example, someone may say, "I would never have guessed she is related to Jim. Their spirit, perspective, and priorities are completely different." If there is nothing of our father in us, who do we resemble, not just by appearance, but by decisions and actions? Perhaps, it is another member of the family or a friend or maybe a mentor or colleague or a teacher or an icon, past or present. It is likely someone who is special to us, who we hold in high regard and in whom we invest our time and energy. It is probably someone we relate to, believe in, and support—whose values we admire and want to emulate and share with others. Some introspection may help identify who we most resemble.

Introspection, however, can sometimes pale in comparison to our capacity for and comfort with passing judgment on others. Christ Jesus shared this truth with these words: "Why do you see the speck that is in your brother's eye, but do not notice the log that is in your own eye?" (Luke 6:41) Even with this verse in mind and trying to uphold it, our tendency may be to minimize our issues while maximizing another's. "After all, we are a good person," we think.

This is part of the parable Christ Jesus shared when He said:

> Two men went up into the temple to pray, one a Pharisee and the other a tax collector. The Pharisee stood and prayed thus with himself, 'God, I thank thee that I am not like other men, extortioners, unjust, adulterers, or even like this tax collector. I fast twice a week—I give tithes of all that I get.' But the tax collector, standing far off, would not even lift up his eyes to Heaven, but beat his breast, saying, 'God, be merciful to me a sinner! (Luke 18:10-13)

Exalting self, judging others, and identifying ourselves as sinners may sometimes come more naturally than introspection. Looking inward with a focus on our foundation, motives, expectations, and the way we care for each other, or the way we do not, may help reveal who we most resemble and are becoming.

Introspection is hard work. It is like using a pick and shovel to break up compacted stony ground to plant a tree. We may dig a planting hole the same size as the tree's root ball, or we may dedicate more time and effort preparing and creating a favorable planting site. The first way can work, but the second way is the one that can improve difficult soil conditions, increasing soil oxygen diffusion, water infiltration and drainage, and aerobic activities and synergism between roots and soil microorganisms. Finishing with a covering of mulch makes conditions for the tree even better.

True, we cannot actually see what is happening below the surface with the roots, but we have a good idea by what is happening above ground, in the part of the tree we see every day, season, and year. The hard work, improving the soil in which the roots grow, makes a difference to its establishment, performance, reaction to adversity, and what it yields through its life.

In the same way, we cannot see the spirit of the heart, but with attention to the log in our own eye, breaking up the compacted and stony soil in our own life, and topping it with genuine affection for people, instead of judging the speck in their eye, the things that our life yields will change, too. Our capacity to do this will come from the soil in which we take root. It will reflect the content of an invisible heart. It will be heard and seen by what we say and do. It will be experienced by those with whom we are connected, and it will testify to the family resemblance we bear.

Keep in mind, however, how easily weeds take root in the soil we have prepared. Sometimes, the weeds use up resources and space, sometimes they make the site unsightly, and other times their aggressiveness chokes out the plants we have sown.

Weed barriers, chemicals, and cultural practices help, but unless we are vigilant and monitor and care for the site and the plants we are growing, the weeds become deeply rooted, producing millions of seeds and reproductive roots that become difficult to contain or remove. Before long a beautiful garden, pasture, or woodland can be overrun with impenetrable and dangerous weeds. Sure, it can be brought back with work and investment, but it is much easier to keep an eye on the garden, protecting it day by day, and pulling weeds as they appear, rather than waiting until they are established, spreading like wildfire and causing damage.

The same is true of our spirit. *The work we do to break up the stony ground can be quickly undone by weeds of distrust, anger, hate, and surrender to old patterns.* Treating someone with respect can be choked by partiality. Providing them support can be buried in hypocrisy. A heart for new beginnings can be crowded out by not letting go of the past. A prayer for someone's salvation can change to forgetfulness by shifting our focus to issues of the day. Unless we keep checking our spirit, perspective, and actions for weeds, and pulling them when they appear, what has been gained can soon be replaced by something we do not want that causes damage and is hard to change.

Some conclude, "If that happens, let's forget about the weeds and change the logo we wear on our shirt and go to work for a company with different values and ways of doing things. That way, we keep working no matter how deep and tangled the weeds get." But the issue is not whether we keep working in the way we always have, but whether we are identifiable with the family we are from and whether we receive, commit to, and fulfill what Christ Jesus has enabled us to do from ages past.

One way to know is by considering who we seek in the watershed moments of our lives and how we respond to their help. In the Gospel of Luke, ten people with leprosy cried out to our Lord, saying, "Jesus, Master, have mercy on us" (Luke 17:13). This brief plea reveals their desperate condition, their need, and their trust. These human beings were isolated from their families, shunned by their communities, and doomed with a fatal disease. Yet, they identified Jesus as Master, the One in charge, who could relieve their suffering and save them.

Jesus said to them, "Go and show yourselves to the priests" (Luke 17:14). What an amazing thing to say. Lepers were not allowed to enter the city, let alone the Temple. They were ceremonially unclean. Jesus could have said, "Okay, I will send the priests to you so you may reenter society with their approval." But that is not what the Lord said, and it is not what the lepers did. The lepers obeyed Jesus and were cleansed.

A Samaritan was one of the ten, a foreigner in the land, not regarded favorably by the society of the day. It was this faithful believer who turned back to give Jesus thanks. Jesus said, "Were not ten cleansed? Where are the nine? Was no one found to return and give praise to God except this foreigner?" And Jesus said to the Samaritan, "Rise and go your way your faith has made you well" (Luke 17:17-19).

Christ Jesus did not ask these questions because he wondered where they were. He knew where the nine were and why they had not returned to give thanks. The questions were not for His sake, but ours. They provide an opportunity for us to determine which of the ten we resemble.

As it turned out, all ten had faith because they all obeyed and were cleansed, but only the Samaritan thought first of Christ. The Bible does not tell us why the nine failed to return. Maybe in their joy over being made well, they ran to family and friends with whom they felt the strongest connection in order to celebrate their recovery and salvation—while overlooking, denying, or forgetting the One who made the celebration possible: the One who provides every heartbeat, every breath and every blessing. The Samaritan may have had family and friends also, but he was not going to them before returning to offer his thanks to God.

Leprosy is like sin, a deadly disease separating us from loved ones, resulting in unimaginable darkness and suffering. But, there is a cure that is portrayed by what the ten lepers said and did, "Jesus, Master, have mercy on us." They knew their disease was costing them their lives. They understood there was nothing they could do to cure themselves. They recognized the Lord Jesus and asked for His mercy and help. Believing and following His Word, they were saved.

The take-away is clear. We cannot buy or earn the cure. It is free for the asking, and it is received by faith in Christ Jesus. It is not dependent on externals: our status among our peers, or what we can do, or what we have done. The Samaritan was a foreigner— he was an outsider and among the most unlikely of people to be reached out to, but, Jesus made him well and blessed him.

Even now, more than 2,000 years after the ten lepers called out to Jesus, we, too, can be stricken with disease and feel like a Samaritan in our own land, in the places we work, attend school, go to church, do business, play, and serve. Even among those closest to us, with whom we thought connections would never fade, we can become labeled, judged, and left out. In Jesus' eyes we are His brothers and sisters who are never forgotten and who He restores to life by His power and grace.

Yet, there are times we may choose to conceal our family resemblance. We may feel it is no one's business, or perhaps we want to minimize risks associated with honoring the One we come from and who we want to be more like. Pressures can also refine and purify. They can bring forth the real spirit of our soul when the layers, defenses, and patterns we have created and accumulated are taken away. It is then that we may truly live in the power and Spirit of God—like Stephen, Peter, Paul, and Timothy did.

It is difficult to lead two lives: one that fits into our times and the other that is devoted to Christ. When we live that plurality, our family likeness may bear little resemblance to Him. That is when our prayers may be ineffective or missing altogether. It is when our job becomes our focus, and family and friends become our foremost joy. It is also when what matters most to us has nothing to do with God.

When we are real, allowing our family resemblance to manifest itself in the way we care and pray for each other—how we serve and forgive without bias or condition—and by our praise for all that our God has done, is doing, and will do (even when we are suffering) that our family likeness shines through.

Perhaps, it is then that we hear our mighty Savior, Christ Jesus, say, "Truly, I say to you, as you did it to one of the least of these my brethren, you did it to me" (Matthew 25:40). Loving His brethren serves Him and shows our connection and family resemblance to Him and with each other. When we are mindful of who we come from—who our words, attitudes, and actions represent—and how we are connected to each other, then our family resemblance is most clearly seen—not necessarily by everyone we are blessed to know, but by some, with whom by God's grace, we find a special kinship. In heaven, it will be unmistakable we have been family all along. Could it be, in that day, we will wonder and regret why it took us so long to see one another as God does: brothers and sisters in Christ? In His likeness, by His love and for our sake He gives us each other.

Family resemblance is something we can embrace or conceal. Perhaps, we do not want to be seen as someone's brother or sister, or as their son or daughter, or their mother or father or as their friend and someone who loves them. The family connection we share is present even in their absence. So, whether by our choice, circumstance, or someone else's influence, a person God gave us to share life with, is not there. If they are dangerous, abusive, or evil, that is not God's will for our lives. If they are not, or if they are changing from whatever the past was, but we refuse to give them another chance, the separation is likely something we have initiated, sustained, or condoned, possibly with no thought of God or them or the family we have cast away.

Remember the words our Lord spoke, *"When you do it to one of the least of these my brethren, you do it to me."* His words were not only about kindnesses we extend, but those we withhold and deny. We may not see each other the way Christ Jesus does: as beloved members of His family, but we can see every person as precious and invaluable to Christ. We can also see one another, whether by blood, by God's grace, or both, as brothers and sisters in Christ. The world will test this view. Heaven will prove it is true. Jesus said, "I am with you always" (Matthew 28:20). This assurance is given so we may know He will never forsake us. Imagine how He must grieve when we forsake each other.

Everyone who has placed their faith in Christ Jesus is a beloved member of His family. He places us together to love and to hold, to protect and to serve, to lift up in prayer, to reach out to in storms, to stand with and for, to share joy and sorrow, and to resemble our Lord who dwells in us. It is not unnatural or difficult to do—but what *is* a struggle is keeping our family identity hidden from the people with whom we share our lives. Guarding what we say and do, avoiding letting anyone know we love Jesus, and pretending to be something we are not can be a lot of work and difficult to do. Worse, it can keep us from fulfilling God's purpose for such a time as this, the place we live, the people we serve, and the sacred stewardship He places in our care.

When we are being real with one another, something of our family heritage and resemblance will shine through. It may be in the way we respond to what happens on the road, or perhaps at work, school, in church, and around the world. It may be the jokes we laugh at, the spirit of words we speak, rumors we share, criticism or hate we harbor, or what we think. It may be what we teach and in what we invest our lives. It may be causes and people we support and those we do not. It may be to embody and share God's grace. It may be all, some, or none of these. But, it will always be that we see in every woman, man, and child God's unique creation and their eternal soul. If this matters to us, it will show up in our thoughts, prayers, deeds, and pattern of living, not only for those we know and love, but for everyone.

Most people will be able to discern what is real and what is behind what we do. Christ Jesus also knows. His Word confirms He knows us through and through. He said, "Why do you call me Lord, Lord and do not do what I tell you?" (Luke 6:46) Outwardly, we may appear to belong to Him, and we and others may believe we do, but inwardly, we may bear little family resemblance to Him because we do not do what he tells us to do. The world looks at the outside and at our past, and comes to decisions about each of us—but *Christ Jesus looks at the inside and knows the truth of our hearts* and what our future holds. He knows our thoughts, imaginings, and deepest desires and what is really behind them all. He knows better than anyone what we do for Him.

Do we bear IIis likeness inside and out? Do we trust His sovereignty without fear and doubt? Do we pray for people in positions of leadership and for one another all over the world? Do we share His love, purpose, and provision for each life He creates? Do we reflect His grace and mercy in what we do for one another, His church, and His glory? Do we long for His return, honoring and remaining faithful to Him in all that we say and do? Our answers are lived out every day and demonstrated by the love and prayers we have for Him and one another. May the Lord's words, "I never knew you" (Matthew 7:23) be heard to our sorrow and separation from our loved ones and Him. Instead, with thanksgiving, may we rejoice together in our Lord's presence with all of our family from eternity past to eternity future—from every nation, tongue, and tribe because the family resemblance we share with each other and Him is so unmistakably clear.

Chapter 8

Well Pleased!

From childhood to old age we are glad when someone notices us for something good—for taking an interest in the person we are—for helping us learn, grow, and realize our potential, and in some way conveying they care about us and are well pleased by what we do. We cherish receiving appreciation for our efforts or, at least, some awareness of the passion and purpose of our heart, and we thrive on encouragement whether we succeed or not. Even the smallest of celebrations for the progress and growth we make inspires us to continue. For restoration of our spirit (something that only our family and closest friends may recognize we need) we treasure counsel that helps us get back on our feet and moving forward again.

It starts with mom and dad and those wonderful words, "I love you. I'm so proud of you." Then a time comes when our teachers, coaches, mentors, and friends may say, "Way to go. You did great." Our spouse and family give us immeasurable joy with the words, "I am so glad you are home. I have missed you." We value our employers, teams, and customers saying, "Thank you." At every stage of life, knowing there is someone who cares or has noticed and acknowledges we have shared something they value, is like receiving a gift from heaven. It is so special when it happens, maybe it is a gift from heaven.

Someone speaking to us with a genuine heart of love, encouragement, and inspiration, not for their benefit, but for ours, may
be giving something far more than kindness. Depending on the
circumstance, timing and application, their uplifting words may
be the affirmation and clarity we have been seeking in prayer
(if what they say is in accordance with God's Word).

There are also people committed to letting us know, in many
different ways, what they don't like. Sometimes, they are the
same people encouraging us one day and correcting us the next.
Moms and dads may do that our whole lives. It is based on their
love and desire for our progress on the course the Holy Spirit
has set us on. Some people are equally committed to telling us,
and others, how displeased they are. They can make it painfully
clear how happy they would be if we were out of their lives
completely. We can distinguish one from the other by their tone,
motive, and means.

The people who simply do not care are the ones we know the
least. They let us do whatever we want. They may recognize
the path we are on is destructive but say nothing. They may not
see the work God is doing in us or care to invest any of their
time or expertise to cultivate our growth. They offer neither
their wisdom nor guidance. We may not matter much to them
one way or the other. There is no telling the impact their help
may have had or how we may have helped them.

All these different people are there by God's providence and
for His purpose. Christ Jesus experienced them all. His apostles and disciples loved Him and by faith followed Him, many
through their own persecution and martyrdom. The Sanhedrin
envied Him, feared Him, hated Him, mocked Him, and ral-
lied the people to shout out, "Crucify Him." (Mark 15:13) The
people of His hometown failed to have faith in Him. His syna-
gogue was blessed by His reading from the book of Isaiah and
a moment later were filled with rage and tried to kill Him. The

government condemned Him, though the governor proclaimed he found no guilt in Him.

It was Peter, who in response to Jesus' question, "But who do you say that I am?" said, "You are the Christ, the Son of the Living God" (Matthew 16:16). Moments later, Peter rebuked our Lord because Jesus told His disciples that He would suffer many things from the elders, chief priests, and scribes and would be killed, and on the third day would be raised. In effect, Peter's protest was telling God in the flesh, standing before Him: you have got this wrong. Jesus answered Peter, "Get behind me, Satan! You are a hindrance to me—for you are not on the side of God, but of men" (Matthew 16:23).

The apostle Peter, who was blessed and corrected within a matter of a few minutes by his Lord, did not see or understand yet that Jesus came, not to live here with us, but that we may live in heaven with Him. "Foolishness!" is what many said then and many say now. They say if He were God He would not have suffered and died to save us. Not only would He, but He did because He, our Creator, immortal and Holy God, is the only one able to take our place, pay our debt, and free us from our sins.

How, in the midst of such pervasive and fearsome animosity toward Him, could Jesus, in His humanity, fulfill His divine purpose? And, how do we fulfill ours? In part, God the Father gives us the answer—twice. When Jesus was baptized by John in the Jordan River, God spoke saying, "This is my beloved Son, with whom I am well pleased" (Matthew 3:17). Again, the Father gave personal witness on the Mount of Transfiguration where He said, "This is my beloved Son, with whom I am well pleased—listen to Him" (Matthew 17:5). How was Christ Jesus able to live and die for us? We will know fully when we meet Him face to face, but we know He focused on pleasing God.

Christ Jesus spoke these words to the people of that time, and to all time, "When you have lifted up the Son of man, then you will know that I am He, and that I do nothing on my own authority but speak thus as the Father taught me. And He who sent me is with me; He has not left me alone, for I always do what is pleasing to Him" (John 8:28-29). To accomplish love in the midst of hate, and to save us from ourselves, Jesus prayed and gave His life completely over to pleasing God, the Father, and doing the Father's will.

In a similar way, our parents are well pleased by us and their love is without end. They forgive us time and time again—they are for us, no matter what—they are overjoyed, even with the smallest of strides we make—they celebrate our lifetime accomplishments and give thanks to God that others see in us what they always knew was there. When we figure this out, something inside us awakens. We want to please our parents or the person(s) who loves us like a parent. That awakening may happen in our youth or perhaps later in life, but whenever it does, we confess our gratitude for their sacrifice and love.

At some point in our life, the desire to be well pleasing extends to our teachers, coaches, friends, employers, spouse, children, and many more. It is good to please those with whom we are connected, who stand with us and on whom we count. Who we seek to please says a lot about us. If we consider all the people we are indebted to and would like to acknowledge in some way, chances are the list is pretty long. There are many people to whom we owe much. Some have helped us realize our dreams, while others have obstructed or denied them and in doing so have made us stronger.

Our list may change based on circumstances and preferences. It is possible some people have moved to another position, while others may have been added. But there is probably someone who has always been at, or near, the top. What is it about her or him that makes them matter so much to us?

Our answers may differ, but there are at least a few similarities we share. For example, the profound connection we have with them, the deep admiration or unwavering respect that increases with time and experience. It may be an abiding trust and assurance that this is the person who has always cared about us, who offers encouragement, counsel, and strength. Or, perhaps, it may be a heartfelt affection or genuine love, apart from physical intimacy, that makes them so important to us.

In addition, all of us may have experienced an awareness of this person's presence in our heart. Perhaps, because everything we think, say, and do matters to them. Some may consider this a part of our conscience, guiding our choices and actions which may be true because they are impacted by what we do. Their presence in our thoughts can provide inspiration and motivation that we are on the right path.

There is a genuine desire to bring them joy. There is something truly amazing about pleasing them, not because of what it means to us, which is a lot, but because of what it means to them, which can be even more. They are our biggest fan, cheering us on as we grow and become what God has always planned. More than anyone, they know about the obstacles and hardships we encountered and overcame and the sacrifices we made along the way. They know because they were there and because they rolled up their sleeves and helped us. They did much behind the scenes, some of which we may never know, like seeking God's protection and blessings for us through their prayers.

Whatever distinguishes the person(s) who matters most to us, there are a few things that are certain: our life is better because they are in it—something about them is irreplaceable—they are the one we look to for guidance and correction—we are blessed by their unwavering love—and they are the one who sees what the Holy Spirit is doing through us for the glory of Christ Jesus. We all need someone like this in our lives. No wonder pleasing them is so important.

Showing them love can take many forms. It may be as simple as sharing a handmade card, providing a note, or just reaching out so they know we care. Perhaps, we share time and interests together on the phone or through a personal visit or a special outing. Whatever it is, the purpose is to convey that, no matter how busy life gets, our relationship with them is a priority we will not take for granted, neglect, or forget. Done from the heart, it can be as welcome and pleasing as God's rain on a hot summer day.

Where does this kind of love that compels us to be well pleasing come from? In part, the apostle Paul provides insight. In his letter to the Galatians, he said, "Am I now seeking the favor of men, or of God? Or am I trying to please men? If I were still pleasing men, I should not be a servant of Christ" (Galatians 1:10). Paul's goal was to serve and please Christ Jesus. This motive, focus, and daily activity is imperative to how we care for our sacred stewardships, and who we turn to for help, particularly when confronted with difficulty, danger and dread.

During the days of Hezekiah, king of Judah, a messenger from the king of Assyria, whose army was conquering every country in its path, brought news saying:

> Do not let King Hezekiah make you rely on the Lord by saying, 'The Lord will surely deliver us—this city will not be given into the hand of the king of Assyria.' Do not listen to Hezekiah; for thus says the king of Assyria: 'Make your peace with me and come out to me—then every one of you will eat of his own vine, and every one of his own fig tree, and every one of you

> will drink the water of his own cistern—until I
> come and take you away to a land like your own,
> a land of grain and wine, a land of bread and
> vineyards, a land of olive trees and honey, that
> you may live, and not die. And do not listen to
> Hezekiah when he misleads you by saying, The
> Lord will deliver us (2 Kings 18:30-32)

The meaning was clear. Jerusalem would be taken and no one could prevent it—not Hezekiah, his troops, or his God. Surrender or there will be war. Scripture says, "Hezekiah rent his clothes and covered himself with sackcloth and went into the house of the Lord" (2 Kings 19:1). These few words convey *grief, repentance, and prayer.* Instead of lifting himself up as the one who would save the day and directing his troops to prepare for battle, Hezekiah's first priority was to humble himself, repent, and consult the Lord.

Imagine: *making God our first option and confessing our sin.* That may take some imagination because recognizing that our strength and defense is in Him—seeking, trusting, and following His Word—and seeing our accountability for sin may not be comfortable or what immediately comes to mind. Sometimes it is only after we have tried everything else, we turn to God. We may think it is our strength and resources, or a person or organization helping us that determines our destiny. Sometimes our focus is so much on our will and our way that seeking God's is unnatural at best or forgotten at worst. Even when we turn to God and pray and are saved by His mercy and grace, we may attribute the result to people and processes other than God's intervention. It is good to be grateful to everyone, but not at the cost of failing to recognize and rejoice in the knowledge that every blessing is from God.

Even when we love and follow Christ Jesus, things happen that can take our attention away from Him and place it on other things. This happened to Martha, the sister of Mary and Lazarus. Martha invited Jesus to her home and was busy preparing a meal for Him. Mary, her sister, was sitting near the Lord listening to what He said. This upset Martha because she was left to make the meal by herself. She asked Jesus, "Lord, do you not care that my sister has left me to serve alone? Tell her then to help me" (Luke 10:40). Jesus answered, "Martha, Martha, you are anxious and troubled about many things—one thing is needful. Mary has chosen the good portion, which shall not be taken away from her" (Luke 10:41-42).

Christ Jesus was not condemning Martha—He loved Martha. His words reminded her, and us, that sometimes the things we do can be so all-consuming and self-important that we forget what matters most. At that moment, Martha was preoccupied with preparing a meal, while Mary was focused on listening to the Lord. Jesus cleared up any confusion about which was needful.

In the book of Job we are given a glimpse of the Spirit of God in a young man whose wisdom exceeded his years. His name is Elihu, the son of Barachel. We know Elihu was younger than Job and those who came to counsel him, Bildad, Zophar, and Eliphaz, because the Bible says, Elihu "waited to speak to Job because they were older than he" (Job 32:4). So he respected their seniority and remained silent until they were through. He was moved to speak because Job had exalted himself instead of God, and his "friends" had no answers and believed Job deserved the agony he was suffering because of sin.

This remarkable young man spoke with a calm demeanor "on God's behalf" (Job 36:2). By the Holy Spirit what he said was clear, convicting, and God honoring. It is interesting to note that when God answered Job in the most extensive narrative from God in the Bible (Job 38–42), without mentioning this young man by name, God made it clear Elihu was right. In contrast, God said to Eliphaz, "My wrath is kindled against you and against your two friends—for you have not spoken of me what is right" (Job 42:7).

King Hezekiah, Martha, and Elihu all had faith in God. Hezekiah displayed it by seeking God in prayer, Martha by asking for Jesus to intervene, and Elihu by testifying of God's glory and sovereignty. A king, a woman of faith, and a youngster connected then, and now, with each other and with us by their devotion to and faith in God. Faith may be something we pray for or want more of in times of special need. Yet, it is not something that is added to us by our condition or need. *It is a gift of the Holy Spirit* that becomes more effective through our application of it and by trusting God.

The Gospel of Matthew provides some examples of faith in action:

> While He (Jesus) was thus speaking to them, behold, a ruler came in and knelt before Him saying, "My daughter has just died—but come and lay your hand on her, and she will live." And Jesus rose and followed him, with His disciples. And behold, a woman who had suffered from a hemorrhage for twelve years came up to Him and touched the fringe of His garment—for she said to herself, "If only I touch His garment, I shall be made well." Jesus turned, and seeing her He said, "Take heart, daughter—your faith has made you well." And instantly the woman was made well. And when Jesus came to the ruler's house, and saw the flute players, and crowd making a tumult, He said, "Depart—for the girl is not dead but sleeping." And they laughed at Him. But when the crowd had been put outside, He went in and took her by the hand, and the girl arose. (Matthew 9:18-25)

98

> And as Jesus passed on from there, two blind
> men followed Him, crying aloud, "Have mercy
> on us, Son of David." When He entered the
> house, the blind men came to Him—and Jesus
> said, "Do you believe that I am able to do this?"
> They said, "Yes, Lord." Then He touched their
> eyes and said, "according to your faith be it
> done to you" (Matthew 9:27-29)

None of these people asked for faith. It was not something they were requesting. It was something they had and were applying. It was not faith in faith, or faith in a group, a place, or an object. *The person and fulfillment of their faith was Christ Jesus.* It is like the man who said to Jesus, "If you can do anything, have pity on us and help us." Our Lord replied, "If you can! All things are possible to him who believes." Jesus changed this man's desperate plea for his son from uncertainty, to the great capacity of faith. The boy's father answered, "I believe—help my unbelief" (Mark 9:22-24).

We all experience crisis, doubt, and fear. These are times the genuineness of our faith can be revealed, not for God's sake because He already knows the truth of our heart and not for someone else's sake, although our trust in the Lord, may influence their life, but for the sake of our relationship with Christ Jesus. Like the father who said, "Help my unbelief," we may discover we need help with that as well. When that happens, remember the words our Lord spoke to another man pleading for his child's life. Jesus said, "Do not fear—only believe" (Mark 5:36).

Something closely connected to our faith that is difficult to do is to wait. It is normal to want answers, progress, and fulfillment. Waiting requires patience, understanding, peace of mind, and trust. Depending on the situation we are in, those things may not be easy to do. In fact, we may wonder where God is, what is He doing, and why He does not come back.

Waiting on God's timing, God's will and His return can test our faith. Keep in mind, while we wait and trust in Him, *He is patiently doing a work in us,* preparing us for what is to come and waiting for us to be ready. So, in a way, Christ Jesus is waiting for us to grow and become who He has made us to be. The difference is, He knows what lies ahead and how to prepare us. At these times in our lives, we may pause, take a deep breath, and consider where we have been, where we are, and where we are headed. Some characterize it as an interlude between the main events of life, others as a time of refreshment and renewal, and some as an opportunity to give thanks to God and to make a decision.

The latter was the case with Joshua, the man God prepared and appointed to lead Israel following Moses' death. Joshua had been at Moses' side for decades. He was one of only two men, Caleb being the other, of twelve people Moses had sent to gather information about the Promised Land. Joshua and Caleb returned with an encouraging report, but the other ten were afraid of what they saw, so they discouraged the people from acting upon or trusting God's Word. The result was Israel did not enter the land God promised Abraham but instead wandered in the wilderness for forty years. Throughout those years Joshua was serving, learning, and becoming what God had planned.

Upon the death of Moses, God said to Joshua, "As I was with Moses, so I will be with you—I will not fail you or forsake you" (Joshua 1:5). Joshua was prepared—he was capable, and he served as God led him, trusting God's Word. Near the end of his life, Joshua called the nation together, paused, and reflected on their history and God's many blessings. He said, *"As for me and my house, we will serve the Lord"* (Joshua 24:15). In that important address, and decision day, he asked his countrymen to choose who they would serve.

We have a similar decision to make. Our Lord explains its importance.

The Gospel of John puts it this way. "Now there was a man of the Pharisees, named Nicodemus, a ruler of the Jews. This man came to Jesus by night and said to Him, Rabbi, we know you are teacher come from God—for no one can do these signs you do, unless God is with him" (John 3:1-2). Nicodemus was a prominent man. He held a position of great power and influence in Israel. Not only was he a ruler of the Jews, he was also a highly esteemed teacher of the Law. Nicodemus would have been sought out by many for his knowledge, guidance, and wisdom and for possessing the definitive and authoritative word on all matters pertaining to life and godliness.

Yet, there he was, seeking an audience with Jesus after the sun had set. Perhaps, he did not want to be seen. What Nicodemus said was not what his contemporaries thought: "We know you are a teacher come from God—for no one can do these signs you do—unless God is with Him." This exceptional man, himself a renowned teacher, called Jesus, Rabbi, a term of deep respect and reverence, in effect voluntarily placing himself under the wisdom and authority of Jesus. What could have motivated Nicodemus to risk so much for a few minutes with our Lord? Jesus answered Nicodemus, "Truly, truly, I say to you, unless one is born of water and the Spirit, he cannot enter the kingdom of God. That which is born of the flesh is flesh, and that which is born of the Spirit is spirit. Do not marvel that I say to you, you must be born anew" (John 3:5-7). Nicodemus answered with a question we may have had, "How can this be?" (John 3:9) Jesus replied, "Are you a teacher of Israel, and yet you do not understand this? Truly, truly, I say to you, we speak of what we know and bear testimony to what we have seen—but you do not receive our testimony. If I tell you earthly things and you do not believe, how can you believe if I tell you Heavenly things?" (John 3:10-12) There it is again: *faith*.

Here is a man that if anyone possessed the outward signs of being heaven-bound, it was Nicodemus. He had all the credentials, all the religion, all the ancestry, and all the prestige. Every human box was checked. Yet, his salvation was not based on his resume, intellect, or accomplishments—it required his new birth.

Nicodemus was drawn to his Redeemer as much for us, as for himself, to receive the answer to the question of his heart about salvation. He returned to his family a changed man. We know he was changed because he did not conceal his next opportunity to be with Jesus, which was to anoint and bury the Lord's crucified body. If social media had existed then, Nicodemus may have set new records for trending with the news that this prominent leader of Israel—a ruler, judge, and teacher—a man of national renown, great wealth, and a star of the Sanhedrin—had given over his heart, service, and life to Jesus of Nazareth, who had been mocked, maligned, convicted, and crucified.

Many in his world may have concluded, and ours as well, that Nicodemus was a fool because of all he walked away from and subjected his family to for publicly aligning himself with Christ Jesus. Others, whose lives have been made new by the Spirit of God, see the blessing of life with Jesus he and his loved ones gained.

The apostle Peter told a suffering church in the first century, possibly with members of Nicodemus' family present, "As the outcome of your faith you obtain the salvation of your souls" (1 Peter 1:9). But, it is not by what they did or by what we do, but by what Christ Jesus has done, and the work of the *Holy Spirit in us when we place our faith in Jesus*.

What are some indications of being born again? Some people can identity and share the exact moment and circumstance of their second birth. Others may not remember the date or details, whether it was sudden like a lightning bolt, or gradual like the emergence of a seed sown in the earth. The confirming evidence of a new birth is change. Jesus said, "That which is born of the flesh is flesh, and that which is born of the Spirit is spirit" (John 3:6). A change has to take place, but how do we determine if we are in the flesh or the Spirit?

One way is by the tone, expectation, and manifestation of our spirit. Is it the same or has it changed? Is our focus on things of the flesh or things of the Spirit of Christ? Are we watching, listening to, talking about, and doing what we have always done, or *have we changed?* Do our fervent prayers to keep a loved one who is dying out of heaven for a while so we can be with them here a little longer, extend to praying as passionately for our unbelieving family, friends, and others that they call on Jesus for their salvation so we can be with them in heaven forever? Has the way we have changed drawn us closer to Jesus, and to each other, or driven us farther away?

Another way is by the fruit of our spirit. The apostle Paul identifies fruit of the Spirit with these conditions and outpouring of the heart: "love, joy, peace, patience, kindness, goodness, faithfulness, gentleness and self-control" (Galatians 5:22). *Does our spirit embody this work of the Holy Spirit in us?*

There is also evidence of new birth by our trust in the sovereignty of God. Failing to understand God's sovereignty is failure to understand and rely upon His capacity and power to do all things, including creating, ordering, sustaining, and restoring all of heaven and earth and everything in them, including all of us. Distrust of this is seen and experienced in the world by our turning inward or disliking or hating someone or something so much that we justify our actions no matter what extreme they take. In effect, we are saying, "I don't know what God was thinking. This cannot be God's will. It does not make sense. We can fix this. We can do it ourselves."

If, or when, we choose this path we may be deliberately or unintentionally overlooking the sovereignty of God, or we may be saying God is not as capable as we thought or that He has lost control or we do not understand or accept His plan or that we believe people and evil can prevail against the will of God or we simply do not believe in Him. Whatever it is, we are making it clear it is the flesh, not the Spirit of Christ, that is in the driver's seat of our lives.

The words of Job spoken to the Lord after all Job had suffered reminds us of God's sovereignty and God's saving grace. Job said, "I know that Thou canst do all things, and that no purpose of Thine can be thwarted" (Job 42:2). All that Job had lost — his family, his health, his home, his wealth, his peace, and more — was restored by the blessing and will of God. Faith is a decision we make — not based on what we see, but in whom we believe.

The apostle Peter said, "Without having seen Him (Christ Jesus) you love Him — though you do not now see Him you believe in Him and rejoice with unutterable and exalted joy" (1 Peter 1:8). In a similar way, the writer of the book of Hebrews says, "Now faith is the assurance of things hoped for, the conviction of things not seen. For by it the men of old received divine approval" (Hebrews 11:1-2). *God is well pleased by our faith in Him!*

Chapter 11 of Hebrews bears witness to many Old Testament men and women of great faith. The chapter concludes by saying, "And all these, though well attested by their faith, did not receive what was promised — since God had foreseen something better for us, that apart from us they should not be made perfect" (Hebrews 11:39-40). This refers to our redemption, made possible by God the Father's plan, by God the Son's sacrifice, and by God the Spirit's work in us.

So the *tone of our spirit, the fruit of our lives, our trust in the sovereignty of God all bear witness to living in the Spirit,* but we cannot be in the Spirit and in the flesh at the same time, and we cannot go back and forth. Our old self passes away when we are made new. The apostle John helps distinguish between the two, "If anyone says, 'I love God,' and hates his brother, he is a liar—for he who does not love his brother whom he has seen, cannot love God whom he has not seen. And this commandment we have from Him, that he who loves God should love his brother also" (1 John 4:20-21). Our brothers and sisters are not only those with whom we align ourselves, but everyone with whom we share the gift of life.

Jesus prayed for us the night of His arrest, testifying of His purpose for our life in the Spirit now and in the life to come. It is great inspiration and guidance for the care of our sacred stewardships and for each other. His prayer is for all time. He said:

> I do not pray for these only (His disciples), but also for those who are to believe in me through their word, that they may all be one—even as thou, Father, art in me, and I in thee, that they also may be in us, so that the world may believe that thou hast sent me. The glory which thou hast given me I have given to them, that they may be one even as we are one, I in them and thou in me, that they may become perfectly one, so that the world may know that thou hast sent me and hast loved them even as thou hast loved me. Father, I desire that they also, whom thou hast given me, may be with me where I am, to behold my glory which thou hast given me in thy love for me before the foundation of the

> world. O righteous Father, the world hast not
> known thee, but I have known thee—and these
> know that thou hast sent me. I have made known
> to them thy name, and I will make it known, that
> the love with which thou hast loved me may be
> in them, and I in them. (John 17:20-26)

Why would God the Son say this, let alone pray it through the power of the Holy Spirit to God the Father? Why express what He already knew? Why ask for the desire of His heart? Why pray that God love us, and be in us and that we be one with them where Jesus is? Full understanding will be one of the many blessings we receive in heaven, but in part this remarkable prayer shares and teaches much about intercessory prayer, faith, and being made new. *From the heart of our Savior, His words reflect His loving and eternal prayers and concern for us.* He teaches us by His prayer that faith must ask with proper motive and believe before it receives and that our new birth is unity with God and each other. Unity of Spirit, nature, will, and love of the Father, the Son, and the Holy Spirit: One.

Oneness is something we know about with our family, friends, work, nationality, God's magnificent creation, and even our favorite teams and celebrities. We become one by virtue of our connection. We cheer one another's success and suffer one another's sorrow. What happens to them happens to us. We share life with them, like no one else. Love for them motivates what we do. We are one!

This is the prayer Christ Jesus lifted up that night and today for us. He knew before our birth, everything that occupies our attention, all of our joys and what unites us and everything that causes division and strife and all the animosity and hate that can destroy people's lives. He has given us the responsibility, through free will, to choose. He prays that our spirit becomes one with His by loving God and all of our brothers and sisters.

To do anything else is reason to consider whether we have been born anew. This choice, this amazing gift from God of free will, does not overlook or excuse the decisions we make—nor does it take God by surprise. Yet, He prays.

Jesus told Simon Peter, "Simon, Simon, behold, Satan demanded to have you, that he might sift you like wheat, but I have prayed for you that your faith may not fail—and when you have turned again, strengthen your brethren" (Luke 22:31-32). Some may think this prayer was misplaced or ineffective because Peter did fail. He denied knowing the Lord. Guilt of this failure drove Peter to weep bitterly. Even before this happened, Jesus knew the result ("when you have turned again"). *Jesus forgave and restored His beloved friend and entrusted a sacred stewardship to him, as He does to us.*

Like His prayer for Simon Peter (with whom we may share "when you have turned again *strengthen your brothers and sisters*"), Christ Jesus already knows the outcome of our lives and faith. We may or may not know, but if in our heart we truly want to please Him, we will focus our attention and daily care for one another on Him.

In evening prayer we may say—"Holy Father, thank You for the miracle and sunset of this day. For every blessing of Your creation and Your gift of salvation I give You praise. Thank You for the sacred stewardship You have placed in my care. I trust it all to You. Please forgive me for what I did and thought that failed to honor You and to lift up my brothers and sisters. I pray there was something of Your love and teaching shared through me today by the leading and power of the Holy Spirit that may have blessed someone and pleased You. For Jesus' sake, Amen."

In the morning, before our day begins we may pray—"Holy Father, thank You for the miracle of Your sunrise and the gift of this new day. For every person You bless me with, I give

You praise. Please light the path I walk with You. I can do nothing apart from You. Forgive me for not remembering precepts You have taught and thank You for Your steadfast love to teach them to me again. Please help me to see my sacred stewardship through Your eyes, to care for it in Your Spirit and to make pleasing and honoring You my highest priority and joy. For Your glory by the power of the Holy Spirit I pray in Jesus' name, Amen."

By God's grace our answer to His call to sacred stewardship will lift up in daily prayer all that He entrusts to our care, fully trusting His sovereign will, giving thanks for His presence and blessings in every hour of our lives and for the incomparable privilege of all He enables us to do *for the love of Christ Jesus.*

Epilogue

A s children, we learn someone believes in us when they entrust to our care a special task, privilege, or gift. Maybe it is a puppy to love or being given permission to ride our bike to school or helping out with household chores. Whatever it is, it begins a new phase of life in which we receive trust, know someone is counting on us, and have a responsibility to fulfill. It is part of growing up and discovering *how we can help make a contribution to God's world.*

It is also a rehearsal of sorts: a season of practice, preparation, development, and making ready for what lies ahead. Perhaps, it is the privilege of being allowed to do more for our family, school, teams we belong to, or for the community or a cause we love. But, it should not be viewed as an audition. We are already in the family, in the school, and on the team. It is not a test, but a blessing and opportunity to hone skills, to be equipped, and to ensure we are ready when God calls.

Sacred stewardships may be sacred rehearsals. Perhaps, for something similar, expanded or different from what we have done. Our previous stewardship and devotion to glorifying God through it will ready us for whatever God ordains to our care in the future.

We need to make sure our focus is fully on what God has entrusted to us now, not on what we may want. *Trust God! "The Lord reigns!"* (1 Chronicles 16:31)

Simon Peter said:

> As each has received a gift, employ it for one
> another, as good stewards of God's varied
> grace—whoever speaks as one who utters ora-
> cles of God—whoever renders service, as one
> who renders it by the strength which God sup-
> plies—in order that in everything God may be
> glorified through Jesus Christ. To Him belong
> glory and dominion for ever and ever. Amen
> (1 Peter 4:10-11)

*May all of our sacred stewardships, entrusted by God, be
served in accordance with His Word: for one another, for His
glory, through Jesus Christ.*

If we ever wonder how, lose our way, or question why, recall the
promise given us when Christ Jesus said, *"Abide in me, and I in
you. As the branch cannot bear fruit by itself, unless it abides in
the vine, neither can you unless you abide in Me"* (John 15:4).

The Author of life is present in us and we in Him. *He will not
fail or forsake us,* and through Him our sacred stewardships will
serve one another for the glory of God. What a great purpose to
fulfill. What a great promise to trust. What a great reason to return
to Jesus, as the Samaritan did, to give praise and thanks to God.

Sacred Stewardships and Trees

Trees and sacred stewardships are created by God.

Each one depends on provisions He provides.

They yield gifts that are shared with others every day.

Both take root and reach upward and outward their whole lives.

They are as strong as the foundation on which they stand.

Both form vital relationships through their lives.

They respond to care and give glory to God.

God's heart and hand is witnessed through us in them.

Each one is a blessing in our keeping for a time.

We plant and water and our great God gives the growth.

CPSIA information can be obtained
at www.ICGtesting.com
Printed in the USA
LVOW10s1923230418
574565LV00010B/76/P